T0271567

Everything is
Going to be
All Right

Everything is Going to be All Right

Poems for When You Really Need Them

Cecilia Knapp

First published in Great Britain in 2021 by Trapeze
an imprint of The Orion Publishing Group Ltd
Carmelite House, 50 Victoria Embankment
London EC4Y 0DZ

An Hachette UK Company

1 3 5 7 9 10 8 6 4 2

A CIP catalogue record for this book is
available from the British Library.

ISBN (Hardback) 978 1 3987 0255 4
ISBN (eBook) 978 1 3987 0256 1

Typeset by Born Group
Printed in Great Britain by Clays Ltd, Elcograf S.p.A

www.orionbooks.co.uk

For my dad, who taught me about hope.

CONTENTS

Chapter 2

Chapter 3

Chapter 4

Chapter 5

Chapter 6

Chapter 7

Credits

Permissions

Foreword

'I lie here in a riot of sunlight', writes Derek Mahon in the poem from which this anthology takes its name, 'Everything is Going to be All Right.' I remember the sensation I experienced the first time I read that poem. It was like a hand reaching out and shifting something within me, so much so that it felt physical. I was briefly in that dazzling ray of light.

This is what good poems do in their own, utterly unique way. Good poems are sharp, bright, and brilliant things that cut right through you. There is something so potent about a poem, these condensed, distilled moments that can take our breath away. They are that hand reaching out. They transport you somewhere else entirely. Sometimes you see yourself within a poem, you jump inside and you move around in there, finding what you need to discover. Often, they are the greatest breeders of empathy. They are a window, opened just a crack, offering you a glimpse of someone else's life. Poems have a unique way of tilting the world and allowing us to see it differently. Sometimes, they give us advice on how to live; they share their wisdom, like Mahon does so well. But I love it too when they ask questions, when they disrupt, when they are scruffy, gritty, un-concluded things that leave us staring at the ceiling. Sometimes there's a sense that the poet is still figuring things out for themselves. The poem becomes a place for discovery. In this way, it reflects the messiness and chaos of living. I find this both comforting and confronting.

Anything can happen inside a poem; it is the land of dreams and adventure. It is an escape. A poem follows its own rules, it delights, as the Frank O'Hara poem I've included in this anthology is testament to: 'Put out your hand, /isn't there/an ashtray, suddenly, there?' How fun is that? How much of an interruption to our every day?

Poems make us feel things. Even if we don't 'understand' them. I've never been of the school of thought that we need to decode a poem to enjoy it; sometimes the way they make us feel is enough, we just ride along with them. Our everyday logic becomes lacking and irrelevant. We transcend it.

When I was putting together this anthology, I wanted the reader, whoever they are – and I believe poetry can and should be for everyone – to be able to pick this book up, turn to a page and feel something; feel that shifting; have their day altered. I know that the poems I've chosen will do this. From old favourites to new voices, this anthology is full of magic.

Take Kim Addonizio's poem 'To the Woman Crying Uncontrollably in the Next Stall,' which I absolutely had to include in this anthology. It's one of the first poems I read that truly activated something in me. I was pretty early into my poetry career and I'd read poems before, loads of them, but there was something about this poem that had a more profound effect. It lingered. Perhaps it was the confidence in the voice; 'Listen I love you joy is coming'. Maybe it was the feeling of being seen. Perhaps it was just the right poem at the right time. But whatever the reason, and I'm not sure it needs to be understood on an intellectual level anyway, it changed me, it moved me in a way I'd not been moved before.

That line, 'Listen, I love you, Joy is coming'; that promise of approaching joy, is what this whole collection of poems hangs upon. It would be remiss of me to ignore the context in which I am writing this foreword. As I type at my kitchen table in the small flat in Hackney I share with my partner and an overweight ginger cat, we are in the throes of the biggest global health pandemic in a century, and one of the most dramatic and disruptive world events my generation has ever seen.

For months, we've stayed at home as health care workers and scientists work tirelessly to battle Covid-19 and front-line workers carry on bravely and diligently trying to keep the world turning in some way. It's a terrifying, cruel and confusing time. We have lost so many people. Vast swathes of industry have declined, jobs have been lost and the future seems uncertain, including for the arts and culture sector as theatre, live music and all the wonderful community arts programmes that benefit so many have ground to a halt.

All this to say; a book that centres joy, that acknowledges our current moment whilst looking to the future, feels like it is needed. Putting this book together, finding the poems that offer hope, that tell us 'Everything is Going to be All Right' has given me solace during one of the most anxious times of my life. It has helped me to rediscover joy and I hope it can help in some small way.

There is so much joy and hope in these poems. There is a marvelling at the world. I'm not suggesting that this book ignores suffering or can irradicate it. As Mahon writes, 'There will be dying'; most of us know that on a deeply personal level. 'Everything is Going to be All Right' doesn't mean 'everything will be perfect.' Rather, Mahon and the poems in this book find means to celebrate in spite of loss, in spite of conflict and pain. They find the beauty underneath. They lean the light and the dark against each other and in this way, they reflect the condition of living. It's no surprise then that stars appear all throughout the book, those little wonders we look up to, reminding us that there's light in amongst the darkness.

There's so much future in this book, the joy is coming, it's waiting to arrive like the sun. 'How can it be that we are just beginning' writes Salena Godden. This is what I turn to in my life most often, the possibility of change. Because for so many of us, and I include myself in this, there have been times when the only thing that keeps us going is the capacity for something different; the belief and hope that we clutch. 'It will be joy from now on' Ocean Vuong pledges. 'When you feel better from this, and you will' Bryony Littlefair writes, 'it will be quiet and unremarkable, like walking into the next room.' The poets in this book show us an alternative, they offer a little sip of something else. They haven't got it all figured out, but their poems are moments of relief.

There is a gratitude and perspective in these poems, a celebration of the small things, everyday adventures that turn the colours of the world up and make everything lush and bright. Vanessa Kisuule's poem 'Chaffinches are sick because' is an exuberant enjoyment of these tiny birds. This is what poems do so uniquely well; they zone in on something and make us see it, really see it with new eyes.

As well as stars, this book is peppered with birds, with sky and flight. And is this not the greatest symbol of freedom, the freedom that self-love allows? 'When I became a bird, Lord, nothing could not stop me,' writes Liz Berry. In a world where self-love is hard to achieve, where it's been commodified to the point of cliché, I hope these poems that reach towards self-love through language will reinvigorate it as a concept and provide a little healing for some. As Rachel Long promises her speaker, 'This time it will be different.' Reece Lyons brings us a powerful insight into her experience as a trans woman and Travis Alabanza asks of themselves 'I wonder all the things I can learn if I try to meet you with love?'

We challenge how we have been taught to see our bodies and the impossible standards women have to meet with Fathima Zahra's 'ode to my thighs' and Maria Ferguson writes with such clarity when she says 'An apple will not save me. Bread is not the villain. /This afternoon I will eat a slice of cake. Tomorrow /I might move my sofa and dance until I sweat.' Mary Oliver tells us 'You do not have to be good.' You can just be you. These poems are like permissions. Give yourself a break; you're remarkable. These poems speak to us.

We look at romantic love in this book too, that vast and sprawling unexplainable thing, the tragedy and the comedy of it. As Richard Scott writes 'Being in love with you is fucking awful.' Love is surely one of the hardest things to write about without wandering into the territory of worn-out tropes. But the poems I've included on romantic love are full of candour, they're unusual, they praise 'Ordinary Sex' (Ellen Bass), they capture that moment when a relationship has ended and you feel clarity, realise that 'the scent of him has lifted/from the last of the sheets.' (Andrew McMillan.)

Perhaps when reading this book, you'll just enjoy the gorgeous buttery feeling of empathy we experience when we read a poem and this will be a little surge of goodness in your day, hearing about someone's mother, my father walking on the hills with his waterproof map, the glorious playground of female friendship, accidentally getting your period all over a picnic rug, dancing, eating, singing all explored on the page. Some of these poems will make you laugh; will make you think, 'me too! I've felt like that before!' These poems will acknowledge you. Selima Hill's 'Cow' is delightfully silly whilst being completely relatable as she wishes to be a 'a queenly cow, with hips as big and sound/ as a department store.' Though it makes us laugh, we also see the truth in it, the sensation of wanting to escape yourself. Sometimes that's the best way to get to a feeling, through the strange and the surreal, through laughter.

But let us look too at grief. Why was it important to me to include these poems of loss? I lost my mum when I was a child and my wonderful brother to suicide years later. What else was there to do but write? To try and find the language to confront this? We all have to meet grief head on, one day. In grappling with our tragedy, or reading about others', are we not saying there is a future for us? That joy is coming? That we will find our own version of Derek Mahon's promise? Are we not saying, *I am moving through it?* Sometimes you need to see your grief reflected back at you in a poem in order to know that you can arrive at a place where you have reckoned with it in some way. Sometimes it helps to feel seen, for the complicated and unresolved aspects of grief to be articulated and for the shame around them to be banished. When we try and grapple with our grief through language, we give our grief a shape, a form to sit inside. Perhaps these poems help us to remember our dead too; 'I am living, I remember you', as Marie Howe writes.

There is a bravery in all these poems. There is a scrabbling towards truth, capturing what our everyday language cannot represent; hope, gratitude, anger, love, loss. I hope you find something in here, something that is like that hand reaching out, some insight on living or the feeling of walking in another's shoes. Like Kim Addonizio reaches out to the stranger in her poem, I want this book to reach out to you; whoever you are, whatever you find here, however you read it, and there is no one 'right way.' Let these poems lift you up, spin you around, hold you.

Cecilia Knapp

Chapter 1

In Spite of Everything, the Stars

EDWARD HIRSCH

Dreams

Hold fast to dreams
For if dreams die
Life is a broken-winged bird
That cannot fly.

Hold fast to dreams
For when dreams go
Life is a barren field
Frozen with snow.

Langston Hughes

In Spite of Everything, the Stars

Like a stunned piano, like a bucket
of fresh milk flung into the air
or a dozen fists of confetti
thrown hard at a bride
stepping down from the altar,
the stars surprise the sky.
Think of dazed stones
floating overhead, or an ocean
of starfish hung up to dry. Yes,
like a conductor's expectant arm
about to lift toward the chorus,
or a juggler's plates defying gravity,
or a hundred fastballs fired at once
and freezing in midair, the stars
startle the sky over the city.

And that's why drunks leaning up
against abandoned buildings, women
hurrying home on deserted side streets,
policemen turning blind corners, and
even thieves stepping from alleys
all stare up at once. Why else do
sleepwalkers move toward the windows,
or old men drag flimsy lawn chairs
onto fire escapes, or hardened criminals
press sad foreheads to steel bars?

Because the night is alive with lamps!
That's why in dark houses all over the city
dreams stir in the pillows, a million
plumes of breath rise into the sky.

Edward Hirsch

"Hope" is the thing with feathers

"Hope" is the thing with feathers -
That perches in the soul -
And sings the tune without the words -
And never stops - at all -

And sweetest - in the Gale - is heard -
And sore must be the storm -
That could abash the little Bird
That kept so many warm -

I've heard it in the chillest land -
And on the strangest Sea -
Yet - never - in Extremity,
It asked a crumb - of me.

Emily Dickinson

For Keeps

Sun makes the day new.
Tiny green plants emerge from earth.
Birds are singing the sky into place.
There is nowhere else I want to be but here.
I lean into the rhythm of your heart to see where it will take
    us.
We gallop into a warm, southern wind.
I link my legs to yours and we ride together,
Toward the ancient encampment of our relatives.
Where have you been? they ask.
And what has taken you so long?
That night after eating, singing, and dancing
We lay together under the stars.
We know ourselves to be part of mystery.
It is unspeakable.
It is everlasting.
It is for keeps.

Joy Harjo

Offerings

for Ông Ngoại

Believe that a hand of bananas
will snag only the purest omens on their tips.
Believe in a powdery bean-moon
wrapped in a cake;
that when I unwind its banana leaf,
I part the earth and return the moon to you.

Believe that our burning papers will reach you
as the finest silk.
Believe that these mandarins are the blaring
shade of wealth, that when peeled
they will glow like the cupped flames
we floated down the Perfume River.

Believe that this pineapple was once a girl
who wished for a thousand eyes,
that it will detect anything that is lost.
Believe that we have learned to split măng cụt
with a meat cleaver,
that their white hearts keep us tender.

Believe that Bà Ngoại has not touched meat

since the last time she saw you,
that she still mutters in Hokkien
although there is no one left who understands.

Believe that we will find you
at the end of this path of salt.

Natalie Linh Bolderston

Happy Birthday Poem

—written the morning of my 48th birthday

and how can it be
that we are just beginning
and not in the middle
but closer to the start
that we hold such hope and faith
when calamity the bass line
and catastrophe the chorus
that when we wake each morning
we reach not for gun and rum
but pen and heart and time
that the party just got started
like yesterday was a dress rehearsal
thank you, the first one was nice
but the next always stronger
and we're not even halfway
and healing is our power
forgiveness is an ocean
and shrinking was an error
and dreaming was a gift
and never giving up
how can it be
we care more now
and love you more than ever
when once death was a space

the end was a destination
and black was not a dress
and sex was not a passport
but learning always sexy
just look at this tattoo we never had
and look at the geography
oh all the places we haven't seen
and all the shoes we never wore
languages unspoken
the science and the nature
the doors that we can open
paintings on the eyelids
this love, this life, my love
how we cannot eat it all
but we stuff our face with laughing
and drink in all the summer
and still stay up too late
and how can it be
we're just getting going
learning to dance
and sing our own tune
that this is just beginning
and change is a constant
and how can it be that
there is more to come

Salena Godden

Thanks

Listen
with the night falling we are saying thank you
we are stopping on the bridges to bow from the railings
we are running out of the glass rooms
with our mouths full of food to look at the sky
and say thank you
we are standing by the water thanking it
standing by the windows looking out
in our directions

back from a series of hospitals back from a mugging
after funerals we are saying thank you
after the news of the dead
whether or not we knew them we are saying thank you

over telephones we are saying thank you
in doorways and in the backs of cars and in elevators
remembering wars and the police at the door
and the beatings on stairs we are saying thank you
in the banks we are saying thank you
in the faces of the officials and the rich
and of all who will never change
we go on saying thank you thank you

with the animals dying around us
taking our feelings we are saying thank you
with the forests falling faster than the minutes

of our lives we are saying thank you
with the words going out like cells of a brain
with the cities growing over us
we are saying thank you faster and faster
with nobody listening we are saying thank you
thank you we are saying and waving
dark though it is

W.S. Merwin

Small Kindnesses

I've been thinking about the way, when you walk
down a crowded aisle, people pull in their legs
to let you by. Or how strangers still say "bless you"
when someone sneezes, a leftover
from the Bubonic plague. "Don't die," we are saying.
And sometimes, when you spill lemons
from your grocery bag, someone else will help you
pick them up. Mostly, we don't want to harm each other.
We want to be handed our cup of coffee hot,
and to say thank you to the person handing it. To smile
at them and for them to smile back. For the waitress
to call us honey when she sets down the bowl of clam
    chowder,
and for the driver in the red pick-up truck to let us pass.
We have so little of each other, now. So far
from tribe and fire. Only these brief moments of exchange.
What if they are the true dwelling of the holy, these
fleeting temples we make together when we say, "Here,
have my seat," "Go ahead — you first," "I like your hat."

Danusha Laméris

God I'm in love with the world today

And I thought about you
And walking hand in hand on a cliff
Covered in green grass
Looking over the sea
On a bright crystal clear day
Holding your small fist tightly in my palm
You chatting so gently and so freely
About all kinds of things
Important things
Frivolous things
And asking questions that you'd asked before
But framing them in a slightly different way
Like, "Dad, is there gravity inside our house?"
And I say "Yes"
But I'm so overjoyed by the question and the way you ask
    it
I could never have asked that question
And I begin to cry because you make me so happy
And the thought of ever losing you would crush me and I
    would no longer exist
Because everything I am or have ever been is wrapped up
    inside of you
Like a sweet chestnut encased in a shell
Then bitten into

Ready to be eaten at Christmas
God how I love to look at you as you stare into the distance
    and dream about Christmas
The joy written in your eyes and dreams
You are my favourite ever thing.

Daniel Cockrill

Poem in Which I Practice Happiness

I love pigeons even
when their claws are stumps
and they walk as though in heels.
I love guinea pigs
for the idea they are in some way
a pig. Their heartbeats make their bodies
vibrate. I like to pretend
to answer them. *Whom may I say is speaking?*
I love football. More people love football
than love social justice
but that doesn't mean football
isn't brilliant. Whenever I head the ball
I feel a poem evaporate.
    I hate the bit of the poem
    where you're obliged
    to hate something.
I love the piano.
I love true crime.
I love the sun
when it arrives
like a tray
of drinks.

Joe Dunthorne

won't you celebrate with me

won't you celebrate with me
what i have shaped into
a kind of life? i had no model.
born in babylon
both nonwhite and woman
what did i see to be except myself?
i made it up
here on this bridge between
starshine and clay,
my one hand holding tight
my other hand; come celebrate
with me that everyday
something has tried to kill me
and has failed.

Lucille Clifton

An Old Story

We were made to understand it would be
Terrible. Every small want, every niggling urge,
Every hate swollen to a kind of epic wind.

Livid, the land, and ravaged, like a rageful
Dream. The worst in us having taken over
And broken the rest utterly down.

                       A long age
Passed. When at last we knew how little
Would survive us—how little we had mended

Or built that was not now lost—something
Large and old awoke. And then our singing
Brought on a different manner of weather.

Then animals long believed gone crept down
From trees. We took new stock of one another.
We wept to be reminded of such color.

Tracy K. Smith

A Litany for Survival

For those of us who live at the shoreline
standing upon the constant edges of decision
crucial and alone
for those of us who cannot indulge
the passing dreams of choice
who love in doorways coming and going
in the hours between dawns
looking inward and outward
at once before and after
seeking a now that can breed
futures
like bread in our children's mouths
so their dreams will not reflect
the death of ours;

For those of us
who were imprinted with fear
like a faint line in the center of our foreheads
learning to be afraid with our mother's milk
for by this weapon
this illusion of some safety to be found
the heavy-footed hoped to silence us
For all of us
this instant and this triumph
We were never meant to survive.

And when the sun rises we are afraid
it might not remain
when the sun sets we are afraid
it might not rise in the morning
when our stomachs are full we are afraid
of indigestion
when our stomachs are empty we are afraid
we may never eat again
when we are loved we are afraid
love will vanish
when we are alone we are afraid
love will never return
and when we speak we are afraid
our words will not be heard
nor welcomed
but when we are silent
we are still afraid

So it is better to speak
remembering
we were never meant to survive.

Audre Lorde

If They Should Come for Us

these are my people & I find
them on the street & shadow
through any wild all wild
my people my people
a dance of strangers in my blood
the old woman's sari dissolving to wind
bindi a new moon on her forehead
I claim her my kin & sew
the star of her to my breast
the toddler dangling from stroller
hair a fountain of dandelion seed
at the bakery I claim them too
the sikh uncle at the airport
who apologizes for the pat
down the muslim man who abandons
his car at the traffic light drops
to his knees at the call of the azan
& the muslim man who sips
good whiskey at the start of maghrib
the lone khala at the park
pairing her kurta with crocs
my people my people I can't be lost
when I see you my compass
is brown & gold & blood
my compass a muslim teenager

snapback & high-tops gracing
the subway platform
mashallah I claim them all
my country is made
in my people's image
if they come for you they
come for me too in the dead
of winter a flock of
aunties step out on the sand
their dupattas turn to ocean
a colony of uncles grind their palms
& a thousand jasmines bell the air
my people I follow you like constellations
we hear the glass smashing the street
& the nights opening their dark
our names this country's wood
for the fire my people my people
the long years we've survived the long
years yet to come I see you map
my sky the light your lantern long
ahead & I follow I follow

Fatimah Asghar

Caught in the Wind

There are things that stick:
the morning quiet accosted by high-strung horns,
the chill seeping into Ahmedabad's December,
blankets wrenched out from hidden pockets
in the high walls of our house,
socks and sweaters swirled into laundry,
rotla crumbled into khaki-coloured soup,
stray dogs tucking themselves deeper
into street corners, and Gauri,
the woman who did the dishes.

Knee-joints long jammed, she'd roll in
on her haunches like a choppy tide.
Cracked-earth hands and weighted breath.
Her husband a red rage most days, and
her sunburnt skin keeping the purples and
greens of his blows a secret.

Her son barring her one night from the house
she'd built. Her setting up camp in the front yard,
daughter-in-law tossing her scraps,
four-year-old grandson growing to regard her
a tumour and refusing her tender calls for her *dikro*.

Gauri hungry. Gauri grazing like a cow for love.
Gauri's failing bones.

But Gauri never wept.
Instead, she'd ease into the wash-pit,
bunch sari into lap and sing:
Lata, Asha, Rafi – the songs she'd
caught in the wind between
houses were hers.

Shruti Chauhan

Grace

That year we danced to green bleeps on screen.
My son had come early, just the 1kg of him,
all big head, bulging eyes and blue veins.

On the ward I met Grace. A Jamaican senior nurse
who sang pop songs on her shift, like they were hymns.
"Your son feisty. Y'see him just ah pull off the breathing
  mask."

People spoke of her in half tones down these carbolic
  halls.
Even the doctors gave way to her, when it comes
  to putting a line into my son's nylon thread of a vein.

She'd warn junior doctors with trembling hands: "Me only
  letting you try twice."
On her night shift she pulls my son's incubator into her
  room,
no matter the tangled confusion of wires and machine.

When the consultant told my wife and I on morning
  rounds
that he's not sure my son will live, and if he lives he might
  never leave the hospital,
she pulled us quickly aside: "Him have no right to say
  that—just raw so."

Another consultant tells the nurses to stop feeding a
    baby, who will soon die,
and she commands her loyal nurses to feed him. "No baby
    must dead
wid a hungry belly." And she'd sit in the dark, rocking
    that well-fed baby,

held to her bosom, slowly humming the melody of
    "Happy" by Pharrell.
And I think, if by some chance, I'm not here and my son's
    life should flicker,
then Grace, she should be the one.

                                        Roger Robinson

Baked Goods

Flour on the floor makes my sandals
slip and I tumble into your arms.

Too hot to bake this morning but
blueberries begged me to fold them

into moist muffins. Sticks of rhubarb
plotted a whole pie. The windows

are blown open and a thickfruit tang
sneaks through the wire screen

and into the home of the scowly lady
who lives next door. Yesterday, a man

in the city was rescued from his apartment
which was filled with a thousand rats.

Something about being angry because
his pet python refused to eat. He let the bloom

of fur rise, rise over the little gnarly blue rug,
over the coffee table, the kitchen countertops

and pip through each cabinet, snip
at the stumpy bags of sugar,

the cylinders of salt. Our kitchen is a riot
of pots, wooden spoons, melted butter.

So be it. Maybe all this baking will quiet
the angry voices next door, if only

for a brief whiff. I want our summers

to always be like this—a kitchen wrecked
with love, a table overflowing with baked goods
warming the already warm air. After all the pots

are stacked, the goodies cooled, and all the counters
wiped clean—let us never be rescued from this mess.

Aimee Nezhukumatathil

Chaffinches are sick because

they don't know about
our manmade terror,
the tyranny of time, or its
cursed opposite: this.
Their song owns the air,
deliberate and gentle
like hand woven lace.
Rah. My flatpack room
is *flooded* with trilling!
Shudder skull an aviary
thick with the threat of
bass and revelation.
Just now, I birthed a
dark, iridescent feather
from my ear canal,
and my fear forget itself.

Vanessa Kisuule

Bath

The day is fresh-washed and fair, and there is a smell of
tulips and narcissus in the air.

The sunshine pours in at the bath-room window and
bores through the water in the bath-tub in lathes and
planes of greenish-white. It cleaves the water into flaws
like a jewel, and cracks it to bright light.

Little spots of sunshine lie on the surface of the water
and dance, dance, and their reflections wobble deliciously
over the ceiling; a stir of my finger sets them whirring,
reeling. I move a foot and the planes of light in the water
jar. I lie back and laugh, and let the green-white water, the
sun-flawed beryl water, flow over me. The day is almost
too bright to bear, the green water covers me from the too
bright day. I will lie here awhile and play with the water
and the sun spots. The sky is blue and high. A crow flaps
by the window, and there is a whiff of tulips and narcissus
in the air.

Amy Lowell

First Blues

That summer night
Was hot
Steaming like a crab
Luscious under the shell

Televisions gone bleary

Blinked
In front of men
In undershirts drinking beer

Wives upstairs took showers
Caught
A glimpse of their backs
In hallway mirrors

I sat in the dark
Invisible
On the backporch
Drinking in the night

And it tasted good
So good
Going down
And somebody like me

Blew night through an alto sax
Blew and blew

His cooling breath
His hot cool breath on me—

And I came alive
Glowing
In the dark
Listening like a fool

Saundra Rose Maley

body weight

[REDACTED] said there was something oddly sexual about
   the way I washed

my feet after getting stuck in a mudflat on Cramond
   Island.

the tide had gone way out and I,
not knowing the sea, or how to swim,

ventured too far off shore.

it was marsh here, for this sand was not solid or ready to
   hold a body's weight.
I stepped too far and it swallowed my right foot,
sandal and all, every inch of sole sucked whole.
when stepping back, my left foot sank in its place.
everywhere was deep, and wet, and in walking back to
   harder ground
the shore refused
to let go.

I relate how I spent what felt like an hour rinsing my feet in
   pools between the pylons
      by the causeway, shaking each foot, kneading straps to
      save the leather.

I don't mention how my feet filled each pool with clay,
   clouds
reclaiming time, clawing back at the clearness of sky.

Gabriel Àkámọ́

Chapter 2

I raised my throat to the
wind and this is what I
sang . . .

LIZ BERRY, BIRD

Bird

When I became a bird, Lord, nothing could not stop me.

The air feathered
                    as I knelt
by my open window for the charm –
                    black on gold,
                    last star of the dawn.

Singing, they came:
                    throstles, jenny wrens,
    jack squalors swinging their anchors through the clouds.

        My heart beat like a wing.

I shed my nightdress to the drowning arms of the dark,
    my shoes to the sun's widening mouth.

                    Bared,
    I found my bones hollowing to slender pipes,
            my shoulder blades tufting down.
        I   spread   my flight-greedy arms
    to watch my fingers jewelling like ten hummingbirds,
    my feet callousing to knuckly claws.
            As my lips calcified to a hooked kiss

silence
            then an exultation of larks filled the clouds
    and, in my mother's voice, chorused:

Tek flight, chick, goo far fer the Winter.

So I left girlhood behind me like a blue egg
                                    and stepped off
                        from the window ledge.

How light I was

as they lifted me up from Wren's Nest
   bore me over the edgelands of concrete and coal.

I saw my grandmother waving up from her fode,
                        looped
            the infant school and factory,
                        let the zephrs carry me   out to the coast.

Lunars I flew

                        battered and tuneless

      the storms turned me insideout like a fury,
      there wasn't one small part of my body didn't bawl.

Until I felt it at last   the rush of squall thrilling my wing
                        and I knew my voice
      was no longer words but song   black upon black.

I raised my throat to the wind
                        and this is what I sang . . .

Note:
charm: birdsong or dawn chorus
jack squalor: swallow
fode: yard

Liz Berry

40

Feast

At your best you are
made-a-wish smoke
of blown out birthday candles.
You are growing up. Grown. Responsible. Sensible.

All of the above.
At your best you are
angel delight, sweet icing girl
At your best you are
lip furled, palms curled, fury hurled.

At your best you are fast;
fast thinking, fast walking, fast everything this world needs
of you. At your best you
lean
back.
Wait for the second or third, forth southbound bus
laugh long, and deep, past curfews calling you home
At your best

you are small on the earth, child you are massive to the
charts, belting hits. You are not short, not tall, not fat, not
thin, not pretty, not butters -- uncontoured chaos
At your best you are; mani-ed, threaded, waxed, and dyed

At your best you are; alive, breathing in a chubby cheek
kind of love

At your best you come apart settle and get swept up, like dust, excellent for delicate work.

At your best you are
a recipe. The home-cooking
of some other rustled up woman who is a concoction of
the kneaded and risen women before them.

Deanna Rodger

Brown Girl

You are a velvet brown butterfly
a delightful puff of afro hair
Intricate cornrows and rope-like plaits
which tiara-sit on top of your head
you are a fragrant lillie on
the cusp of blossoming
a rainbow of brilliant colours
dazzling and mesmerising.

You are a delicious and moist
triple layer chocolate cake
the kind you have on a birthday
covered in candles and multi-colored sprinkles
you are the uncontrollable giggles
of a thousand girls who laugh until their bellies hurt
until tears of happiness flooded down their faces
and they are afraid they'll wet themselves.

You a fluorescent green
hula hoop whipping around a waist
an energetic skipping rope, jump, jump, jump
you are pink, you are blue, you are neither
you are solid mountain
you are whirling hurricane
you are all shades of brown from
midnight blue to the lightest shade of caramel.

You are up late-night reading your favourite book
the red glitter pen in the middle of a messy bedroom
the sweet taste of strawberry flavoured bubblegum
the secret writing in your diary
you are the buzz of a fat bumble bee
the soft feathers of a baby robin
the tiny miaow of a snuggly kitten
the soft lapping of a retreating tide.

You are popcorn popping in a microwave
a whirling cartwheel in a playground
a wobbly handstand against a school wall
you are the chalk used in Hopscotch
an uncontrollable pingy bouncy ball
you are a gaggle of girls, hip to hip, hand to hand.
secretly whispered whispers
the sweet aroma of possibility.

Kat François

#GirlsLikeUs

We are the girls who serve fantasy at the self-service
  checkout in Sainsbury's,
who are the definitions of an unexpected item in the
  bagging area.
We are the girls with something extra.

Girls like us
who possess a walk that is fit for the gods,
one that stops traffic as we strut past,
we are the girls who carry sass in our steps
and always turn heads.

Girls like us
who are the hot girl summers
dreaming of the day we can bathe on beaches
unbothered
free to re-enact our own episodes of Baywatch
replace the convention of Pamela Anderson with

Girls like us
who are untouched,
never had our hands held in the light
mistake fumbling palms for desirability,
we are the girls who were never taught how to
  acknowledge our beauty
because boys were not meant to be beautiful.

Girls like us
who are never considered to be 'girlfriend material'
even though,
we are hot as fuck.
Instead we are made from loose seams,
always breaking free from the fabrics of our flesh,
a Sari worn by the Hijra Community,
the feather headdress adorned by Two Spirits
to the stiletto heels we flex in the city
we are the girls who never learned of our histories.

Girls like us
who find sisterhood within a hashtag,
we are the 'Am I trans enough' girls,
the 'I know I'm trans but I'm too scared to come out yet'
    girls,
us who are questioning and us who are stealth,
us with supportive families and us by ourselves.
Us who have learned how to wear pride on our sleeves
and Trans with a capital T.

Girls like us
who's blood stains television screens every month
girls like Naomi Hersi and Claire Legato,
girls like Muhlaysia Booker and Chynal Lindsey.

Girls like them
who are no longer with
us

and all of the others,
who are a symphony of unsung eulogies,

the ones who are misgendered in police reports,
who never make it to the news headlines,
we are justice for the murders gone unrecognised.

Girls like us
who are still here against all odds,
the sound of our heels clicking onto concrete is a
    celebration.
A reminder that we are still walking that walk, fit for the
    gods.

Girls like us
who you will find in the rubble of the construct,
that we tore down with nothing but our bodies,
what gender will your ash be when you burn

just like us?

Reece Lyons

Love Poem to Myself

after Jack Underwood

your hair continues to surprise me in its texture after every
single wash / like the shock of a photocopier lid realising
the other side when it beams white light / I could listen to
you listing your banned foods for days / and tell you bad
jokes about music as the food of love for even longer / if
I pause to consider how long it takes nurses to find your
veins / I too blush with warm pride and joy / your ears are
unremarkable / and therefore impossible to improve /
when I chance upon your face in the curvature of a kettle I
am overcome by the urge to blow you kisses / as if we are
both tethered to the ground / but neither of us want to
take off

Cia Mangat

48

For when my body does not feel right

To be spoken out loud after you have looked in the mirror.
To be spoken out loud after those mornings where you
can tell things are not aligned.
To be spoken out loud after someone has misgendered
you despite knowing you for years.
To be spoken out loud after you have accidently
misgendered yourself.
To be spoken out loud after you have purposefully
misgendered yourself.
To be spoken out loud after the dress you thought would
fit did not.
To be spoken out loud after the stubble starts to feel too
much of a shadow.
To be spoken out loud after someone has shouted _____
at you on the street.
To be spoken out loud after you have whispered _____ at
yourself.
To be spoken out loud after you have sex that doesn't
maybe feel good.
To be spoken out loud after someone tried to tell you that
you are not real.
To be spoken out loud after you try to run away from
someone.

To be spoken out loud after you try to run away from
    yourself.
To be spoken out loud after you come back home.
To be spoken out loud after a scratch or a bruise may hurt
    you.
To be spoken out loud after you may scratch or bruise
    yourself.
To be spoken out loud after someone tries to shrink you.
To be spoken out loud after you try to shrink yourself.

To be spoken out loud.
Loudly.
Whenever after may fall:

> To hate yourself and to think you are wrong
> Is the only consistent education we have all had.
> It is a thankless task that leads to block roads.
> It is a procrastinator that will only end in more
>   unrest.
>
> I do not hate you. I hate what has been told to you.
> I do not hate you. I hate who is around you.
>
> I wonder all the things I can learn if I try to meet you
>   with love?

Travis Alabanza

ode to my thighs

if we could pick out thighs like Christmas trees
from the Sunday market, you wouldn't be
my first choice. o stretcher of size 8 pants. o pear
shaped criminal. o shame in jeans. o thick
tendrils. you, not-even-cute thighs. when the boy in
the book I'm reading gets run over by a car & he
wakes up, I feel each screw drilled in, the
searing pain, and at night, my hands slide under
the covers to see you haven't left me. I am
a terrible owner, I'll admit. I don't let you swim
as often or move in a dress the way people
do in movies. o map for a lover's fingers, pay
no attention to the mirror curses I send your
way or the voices of middle school girls' laughter,
they didn't know love like this.

                                        Fathima Zahra

Hymn

It's one of those days where you've found God, finally.
You've been heathen for weeks

but now your body—
its mottled legs, its fingers gripping the kettle

—now your voice, its own animal, belting out
Dolly in the garden you're lucky to have

—now your mood, reflecting off red brick terraces,
and painting the pavement in light

have brought you in under the wing of religion.

It's one of those days where God's right here,
not bearded or sandaled, not a bloke in a robe,

just your body, walking uphill to the park.

Jemima Foxtrot

Responding to a Crisis

I am waiting for the butter to soften so I can bake
a Victoria sponge. The most I'd baked before this
was a spud. Isn't it funny what my body does?

I have unanswered emails and unfinished
pages but my plants are alive and my bathroom
is sparkling. I want so badly to hug my mum.

An apple will not save me. Bread is not the villain.
This afternoon I will eat a slice of cake. Tomorrow
I might move my sofa and dance until I sweat.

My body is amazing. Spilling over
this bed with nothing to do but wait.
I've decided to make an oven of it.

Maria Ferguson

You Know a Market Where the Tulips are Still Three Quid

and you buy them to remind yourself that you can.
They begin tight-lipped and upright,
but their petals become loose, droop.
Their stems will start to lean away from their own.
You know the cat will cry at two AM,
some nights you will sleep right through,
others your body will fling you upright as though
your brother is dying. You know what the wine does to
   your teeth.
You know about leaving.
You know you keep useless things
in case you need to build a shrine.
You know how to make gods of men
whose toothbrushes sit caked on the counter.
You know this, and you let them weigh your avocado,
rolling it around in their palm.

Cecilia Knapp

Megan Married Herself

She arrived at the country mansion in a silver limousine.
She'd sent out invitations and everything:
her name written twice with "&" in the middle,
the calligraphy of coupling.
She strode down the aisle to "At Last" by Etta James,
faced the celebrant like a keen soldier reporting for duty,
her voice shaky yet sure. I do. I do.
"You may now kiss the mirror." Applause. Confetti.
Every single one of the hundred and forty guests
deemed the service "unimprovable."
Especially the vows. So "from the heart."
Her wedding gown was ivory; pointedly off-white,
"After all, we've shared a bed for thirty-two years,"
she quipped in her first speech,
"I'm hardly virginal if you know what I mean."
(No one knew *exactly* what she meant.)
Not a soul questioned their devotion.
You only had to look at them. Hand cupped in hand.
Smiling out of the same eyes. You could sense
their secret language, bone-deep, blended blood.
Toasts were frequent, tearful. One guest
eyed his wife — hovering harmlessly at the bar — and
imagined what his life might've been if
he'd responded, years ago, to that offer in his head:
"I'm the only one who will ever truly understand you.

Marry me, Derek. I love you. Marry me."
At the time, he hadn't taken his proposal seriously.
He recharged his champagne flute, watched
the newlywed cut her five-tiered cake, both hands
on the knife. "Is it too late for us to try?" Derek whispered
to no one, as the bride glided herself onto the dance floor,
taking turns first to lead then follow.

Caroline Bird

Cow

I want to be a cow
and not my mother's daughter.
I want to be a cow
and not in love with you.
I want to feel free to feel calm.
I want to be a cow who never knows
the kind of love you 'fall in love with' with;
a queenly cow, with hips as big and sound
as a department store,
a cow the farmer milks on bended knee,
who when she dies will feel dawn
bending over her like lawn to wet her lips.

I want to be a cow,
nothing fancy –
a cargo of grass,
a hammock of soupy milk
whose floating and rocking and dribbling's undisturbed
by the echo of hooves to the city;
of crunching boots;
of suspicious-looking trailers parked on verges;
of unscrupulous restaurant-owners
who stumble, pink-eyed, from stale beds
into a world of lobsters and warm telephones;
of streamlined Japanese freighters
ironing the night,

heavy with sweet desire like bowls of jam.

The Tibetans have 85 words for states of consciousness.
This dozy cow I want to be has none.
She doesn't speak.
She doesn't do housework or worry about her
    appearance.
She doesn't roam.
Safe in her fleet
of shorn-white-bowl-like friends,
she needs, and loves, and's loved by,
only this –
the farm I want to be a cow on too.

Don't come looking for me.
Don't come walking out into the bright sunlight
looking for me,
black in your gloves and stockings and sleeves
and large hat.
Don't call the tractorman.
Don't call the neighbours.
Don't make a special fruit-cake for when I come home:
I'm not coming home.
I'm going to be a cowman's counted cow.
I'm going to be a cow
and you won't know me.

Selima Hill

Deliverance

I've known it from the day
he were born.

I were in the hospital
and the midwife put him on my chest
and I held him
and I felt him
you know, *felt* him

and I says to myself

I says
Joanne

this baby
is a gay
a gay baby.

And I just thought

well
that's that.

I love him
no different.

That's that.

Toby Campion

Pride

I am seventeen, summer is still gold clap of hot body
and hot body. Blue sky fries the tiny sun.
I kiss myself for courage and duck into the parade.
Two dykes smiling like young mothers ask me my name.
Our gazes lock on love, our slow went among the cut offs,
wrecked docs, glinting nose rings, head shaved to skin,
a stranger's head on my shoulder became a loving mouth
pressing its heat into mine, urgent tongue searching for a
    place
to pass the root in that way, to go knuckle deep in another,
in a third way sucking white sap directly
and watering the teat, going out unshowered but for that
    fresh sweat –

am I the steaming black street, am I the banner and the
    band, the crush,
lilting ale, tipsy hug, charged flesh and open eye.

That was then heading to First Out when it was us on the
    menu,
salad of fierce look and full power lasagne, speaking with
    full mouth:
queer, lesbian, dyke. Offender of no gender. Failed woman.
Swamp. Black flag. Bleach blonde. Sunday Happy Sunday.
What it was to me then, those bare arms, to have found
    them at last,

below a slow float, that heat, that mood, that pride.

My body taps me on the heart when someone in soft
   leather swims
into my ken, that smell of squat and underground and
   every other lover,
scent that throws off shame – these days I pass you in the
   street,
though I want to turn around and thank you for the tongue
   in my throat,
for this thick and practiced ass and cunt, for my plaited
   scars and flat nipples

They call this a city, I call it the dark between two bodies.

Jay Bernard

The Yearner

I stacked three pillows, made sure
my head was heavy with bills, wine, yesterday's
deadline, and I slept hard, tight
as cement on my left arm. The needles came.
At dawn, I dragged it
like a salmon from under my body.
A part of me is dead. Now
I can shake my own hand,
meet myself again for the first time.
How my fingers feel to one another, strangers,
for a tingling moment, I am another.
Promise? This time will be different.

Rachel Long

Chapter 3

*I promise
they were absolutely
ruined by its magic*

MARK WALDRON

That's My Heart Right There

We used to say,
That's my heart right there.

As if to say,
Don't mess with her right there.

As if, don't even play,
That's a part of me right there.

In other words, okay okay,
That's the start of me right there.

As if, come that day,
That's the end of me right there.

As if, push come to shove,
I would fend for her right there.

As if, come what may,
I would lie for her right there.

As if, come love to pay,
I would die for that right there.

Willie Perdomo

Trees

Somebody told me once that perfect love
is two trees growing side by side
in their own time, never leaning on the other one.

I think that sounds bloody lovely,
but it doesn't actually happen like that.

If you ask me, love is wasps and grasshoppers.
It's anger, patience and stings and finding the legs
to jump into things and get stuff done.

Today is another duvet day, we read stale news
and stay indoors. We talk less, cuddle more,
remember when our legs did all sorts.

Outside our cluttered bedroom, the council
are chopping at the London planes,
they have to hack them back to make more space.

As they drop one by one onto the pavement,
I think, *pretty soon we will be light and air again.*

Laurie Bolger

Underneath the Gone Sky

They stood, stretched with relief and fear,
   the spilt night over everything.

The wall she was against was on the world's edge,
   her back against her shirt, her shirt against her coat,

her coat against the brick, its knuckle grit holding her on.
   And beneath unspeaking clothes, he found her

ludicrously bare, peaceful, shocked,
   as though her clothes had been her skin

her skin, flesh. I promise
   they were absolutely ruined by its magic.

Mark Waldron

For Grace, After a Party

You do not always know what I am feeling.
Last night in the warm spring air while I was
blazing my tirade against someone who doesn't
interest
       me, it was love for you that set me
afire,
       and isn't it odd? for in rooms full of
strangers my most tender feelings
                       writhe and
bear the fruit of screaming. Put out your hand,
isn't there
       an ashtray, suddenly, there? beside
the bed? And someone you love enters the room
and says wouldn't
       you like the eggs a little
different today?
       And when they arrive they are
just plain scrambled eggs and the warm weather
is holding.

Frank O'Hara

For I Will Consider My Boyfriend Jeffrey

*after Christopher Smart's Jubilate Agno, Fragment B,
[For I will consider my Cat Jeoffry]*

For I will consider my boyfriend Jeffrey.
For he is an atheist but makes room for the unseen,
  unsayable.
For he is a vegetarian but makes room for half-off Mondays
  at the conveyor bely
    sushi place.
For he must vacuum/mop/scrub/rinse/hand sanitize/air
  freshen the entire
    Apartment to deal with the stress of having received a
  traffic ticket.
For he dances in his seat while driving us to the
  supermarket.
For he despises tarantulas, sharks, flying on planes, &
  flightless birds such as the
    cassowary of New Guinea, which he has only seen in
  videos & thinks looks
    like a "goddamn velociraptor."
For he likes to claim he is the butch one.
For he is Jeffrey Gilbert of Gilbertsville, New York.
For he lets his beard grow.

For when his beard has grown up & own & out, he takes a
    tenderly long time
        to shave.
For this he performs in ten steps.
For first he looks upon his furry countenance to assess &
    accept the difficult
        journey that lies before him.
For secondly he washes with holistic care his whole foxy
    face.
For thirdly he applies as much shaving cream as I use in a
    month.
For fourthly he puts on Erik Satie or LCD Soundsystem.
For fifthly he sways a little, to the music, before lifting to
    his cheek the buzzing
        razor.
For sixthly he shaves.
For seventhly he shaves.
For eighthly he shaves.
For ninthly he shaves, then asks me to come help.
For tenthly he holds back a giggle while I tickle the back of
    his neck with the
        buzzing razor.
For having shaved, he declares that he is ready to get back
    to work.
For his work involves many instruments, including a large,
    completely
        unnecessary keytar, or keyboard guitar, which he
    plays beautifully.

For he plays & then transfers his playing onto a computer,
    where he works on it
        further.
For he wears big headphones like little moons on his ears
    & begins to bounce
        in his chair for the room is becoming a continent of
    rhythms & almost-
        meanings & just-discovered birds only he can hear.
For though he does not fare well on planes he will fly to
    those he loves.
For his beard is already growing back.
For he looks happy & doesn't know I'm looking & that
    makes his happiness free.

Chen Chen

The Distance of Me

It wasn't Valentine's Day so there was no pressure to take
   part in such an activity
But we were talking about veins and inspecting each
   other's hands
It came to my attention that I don't actually know the back
   of my hand that well
I'm sure the back of someone else's hand looks quite
   similar to mine
Saying that, I think I probably would be able to pick the
   back of my hand out in a police line up
"Do people have veins in the same places?" She asked
"Oh you've got one there, I've got that one there too look."
Comparing our natural networks
"No I haven't got that one. My version of that one is there
   on me I think."
We got onto blood and the internet
Learning that an adult body has an average of 5.6 litres of
   blood contained within it
Circulating round the body three times every minute
In one day the blood travels 19000 km or 12000 miles
Numbers coming into view of someone like me having up
   to 100,000 miles of blood vessels in them
It seemed like a convenient number to me

But yes if you took all the blood vessels of an average
adult and laid them out in one line, the line would
stretch over 100,000 miles
Makes me feel loaded, surely I could spare a few metres for
some Spiderman style wrist webs
The sprawling branches of our interior maps
Cutting down a forest and meticulously sticking every
single branch of each tree and the trunks together from
end to end to see how long the forest stretches
Every tiny twig going in a different direction
Cut into a measurable length
How long is that forest?
What do you mean? How long does it take to walk through
it?
No I mean if you chopped all the branches and trunks into
a length and stuck them together how long would it be?
Longer than all the blood vessels in a human body?
Walking through Epping Forest I wonder "would this forest
stretch out further than my blood vessels? Probably not
I've got 100,00 miles in me."

Rob Auton

After Making Love in Winter

At first I cannot have even a sheet on me,
anything at all is painful, a plate of
iron laid down on my nerves, I lie there in the
air as if flying rapidly without moving, and
slowly I cool off—hot,
warm, cool, cold, icy, till the
skin all over my body is ice
except at those points our bodies touch like
blooms of fire. Around the door
loose in its frame, and around the transom, the
light from the hall burns in straight lines and
casts up narrow beams on the ceiling, a
figure throwing up its arms for joy.
In the mirror, the angles of the room are calm, it is the
hour when you can see that the angle itself is blessed,
and the dark globes of the chandelier,
suspended in the mirror, are motionless—I can
feel my ovaries deep in my body, I
gaze at the silvery bulbs, maybe I am
looking at my ovaries, it is
clear everything I look at is real
and good. We have come to the end of questions,
you run your palm, warm, large,
dry, back along my face over and
over, over and over, like God

putting the finishing touches on, before
sending me down to be born.

Sharon Olds

2 Become 1

You are slowly running your hand along my waist
and I am so aware of my breathing and your fingertips
and the hair on your face that skims the inches of my
shoulder blade that I wonder if our bodies
are the same now, or

maybe in the magic space between night and day –
the space only people who have people understand,

maybe at some time before the dawn we were so close
to one another we became the same person
and we either did not realise or we simply did not care.

Bridget Minamore

Psalm 150

Some folks fool themselves into believing,
But I know what I know once, at the height
Of hopeless touching, my man and I hold
Our breaths, certain we can stop time or maybe

Eliminate it from our lives, which are shorter
Since we learned to make love for each other
Rather than doing it to each other. As for praise
And worship, I prefer the latter. Only memory

Makes us kneel, silent and still. Hear me?
Thunder scares. Lightning lets us see. Then,
Heads covered, we wait for rain. Dear Lord,
Let me watch for his arrival and hang my head

And shake it like a man who's lost and lived.
Something keeps trying, but I'm not killed yet.

Jericho Brown

love version of

tonight I watched you sleep
naked on the futon
face down sweaty like a small child
and knew that everything else was bullshit

it's so hard to stay alive these days
or sane
so keep on snoring danny
while I guard you like a rottweiler

being in love with you is fucking awful
cause one day you'll stop breathing
in this grey light you already look dead

but then you smile thank fuck
what are you dreaming about baby wake up
tell me if the word soul still means anything

Richard Scott

78

Love

The way you hold your cup in a closed fist
Your wrists that get rheumatic in the rain
Your long feet, long legs and bony shoulders
Your smile a crash of teeth from nose to chin.

Your eyes drop three octaves when you want me
Your body is transposed into the key
Of sand dunes, raw quartz, heat from a slow sun.
Suddenly as graceful as when you dance
No longer smashing your limbs into
Unmoving table-tops or burning your hands
On every available hot surface
Or head-butting the car door when you dive in

You know, it used to keep me up at night,
The lack of you

Kae Tempest

While the Child Sleeps, Sonya Undresses

She scrubs me until I spit
soapy water.
Pig, she smiles.

A man should smell better than his country—
such is the silence
of a woman who speaks against silence, knowing
silence moves us to speak.
She throws my shoes
and glasses in the air,

I am of deaf people
and I have
no country but a bathtub and an infant and a marriage
  bed!

Soaping together
is sacred to us.
Washing each other's shoulders.

You can fuck
anyone—but with whom can you sit
in water?

                                        Ilya Kaminsky

Ordinary Sex

If no swan descends
in a blinding glare of plumage,
drumming the air with deafening wings,
if the earth doesn't tremble
and rivers don't tumble uphill,
if my mother's crystal
vase doesn't shatter
and no extinct species are sighted anew
and leaves of the city trees don't applaud
as you zing me to the moon, starry tesserae
cascading down my shoulders,
if we stay right here
on our aging Simmons Beautyrest,
dumped into the sag in the middle,
that's okay.
You don't need to strew rose petals
in my bath or set a band of votive candles
flickering around the rim.
You don't need to invent a thrilling
new position, two dragonflies
mating on the wing. Honey,
you don't even have to wash up after work.
A little sweat and sunscreen
won't bother me.
Take off your boots, babe,

swing your thigh over mine. I like it
when you do the same old thing
in the same old way.
And then a few kisses, easy, loose,
like the ones we've been
kissing for a hundred years.

Ellen Bass

fifteen

with a hopscotch grid for a wrist
see my sad boy

with a smile like a one-string guitar
relative to nobody, yet out of tune

dropping out of school
out of line, saying *I love you*

more than life itself
in a first Valentines card

during the spring term
in which we turn fifteen.

in the attic of an old phone, now
here he is again

in a drawer I was cleaning out
in a game I was winning

until I met him
& here he is, my sad boy –

now watch this older girl stop
& cast her day out in the dust

& grow sad too.
this whole impermanence thing is deceptive.

looks lifelong, actually, to me

sat here, still moulding mason jars
of words to preserve him with;

wondering if a poem ten years on
is still a pining; asking

how many more of these I will make
before I learn how little of us lasts.

Victoria Adukwei Bulley

A series of statements

After Franny Choi

we good?

It's important to remember that sometimes
to be good is not a one step process.
Being good, in this context a synonym of being okay,
is a performance you wear every day.
Consider it as part of your morning routine
before work, like taking your vitamins
or making sure you get the right bus
at the right time, 319 at Kings Road
at exactly 8:18am or else
you'll feel ill or missing,
like a part of you was left untaken.

/I hope you've found someone good for you

Sometimes in moving too fast
the gaps blur with the rest of the concrete,
and jumping over them
becomes too much of a human task.
In the middle of this accelerated state,
we cling onto any love that is offered
before we truly want them,
let the juice stick on our fingers,
not fully understanding how it tastes.

/please don't leave

How funny to look back
on the people we've failed to hold onto
and the result is this: a version of ourselves
whole in one conversation,
fragments in the other, pieces generating
cells around themselves,
working on something new.

Troy Cabida

Then

For the first time, I listen to a lost
and secret recording of us
making love near-on ten years ago.

I recognize your voice, your sounds,
though if I knew no better,
I could be any man in any room.

After, the rising sounds of rising
and of dressing and once
as you step up close to the deck,

perhaps to pick up shoes, you sing
the chorus of *Sunday Morning*.
I call on you to hurry and we leave.

It does not end then; the tape rolls on.
A few late cars which sigh by
might have passed us walking away

triumphant, unaware we've left behind
this mop and mow mechanism
of silence to which we may never return.

Roddy Lumsden

I'll Open the Window

Our embrace lasted too long.
We loved right down to the bone.
I hear the bones grind, I see
our two skeletons.

Now I am waiting
till you leave, till
the clatter of your shoes
is heard no more. Now, silence.

Tonight I am going to sleep alone
on the bedclothes of purity.
Aloneness
is the first hygienic measure.
Aloneness
will enlarge the walls of the room,
I will open the window
and the large, frosty air will enter,
healthy as tragedy.
Human thoughts will enter
and human concerns,
misfortune of others, saintliness of others.
They will converse softly and sternly.

Do not come anymore.
I am an animal
very rarely.

Anna Swir

All My Ex-Boyfriends are Having a Dinner Party

1–

comparing their tight obliques,
how red their meat, hattricks
for their grassroots teams,
wearing expensive suits,
saying they had me in a car once,
how I can never kept my mouth shut,
I always wanted to stay the night.
I'm dieting again, sipping
low cal miso,
burning my hands
on a moving train.
I smile at other joggers,
I'm enjoying this.
The dentist says
I have yellow teeth,
his hands hold my tongue.
Mum said you can do anything
as long as you're wearing
washing up gloves.

2-

A purple leaflet in the waiting room
asked me if life has worked out
a) better
b) worse
c) the same
For one thousand pounds
I can fix my teeth.
Mum used to ballroom dance
with a wooden spoon,
weeping with the radio.
I've been keeping my fallen eyelashes in a bag,
I spit pink foam into the sink,
decide this week I'll only eat eggs
until the days smudge.
Pain is a man in a blue suit.
I see people eating crisps in public
on a Monday
like they have no guilt.

Cecilia Knapp

Finally

a day will come   when
woken by the xylophone
of sunthroughblinds
you'll realize

that the beach was not the place
where horses tore the sand
to ribbon

that the scent of him has lifted
from the last of the sheets
that he isn't coming back

that it hasn't rained
but the birds are pretending that it has
so they can sing

Andrew McMillan

Chapter 4

I've been thinking: This is what the living do

MARIE HOWE

LOROS

I watched my mother form
her new body. Cheekbones becoming violent,
hips clucking to meet skin.
I would wash her as she used to wash me,
holding a small plastic jug
under the warm water
and tipping it over her back,
her edges broken by bubbles.

That night was like any other night
in the hospice. People quietly dying,
except we ate ham and pineapple pizza
in her bed. Watch out for the men, she said
they have the upper hand. She smelt salty,
shoulders poured against a medical pillow.
The next day, when the doctor said she needed

to eat more, she laughed,
told him she had waited forever to be
this thin. I laughed with her.
When I try to replay her voice,
I can't. This small slice is what I have.
A woman happy with her own shrinking
in the last weeks of her life.

Cecilia Knapp

18th of November

In our mother's garden only a few leaves
      are left now and the sun is quivering
    through the branches. Happy Birthday,

brother boy. Are you already eight months gone?
      We measured days like our mother
    measures rice methodically in the dent

of her palm. Last night I dreamt of our childhood
      home, filled with spectral figures
    only the furniture was vivid, and you.

You'll want to know that the garden has been
      kind to us, because the house has not.
    From here, by our old swings, how easy it is

to forget and to see you stepping outside to the patio
      blinking behind your spectacles,
    on the 18th of November, your birthday
    a newspaper dangling from your hands.

Mona Arshi

Back up for the Funeral

driving up the road
as pinks and blues collide
  a sky like sleeping beauty's dress

in the best part of the film
– colours flicking back and forth
between the fairies' magic wands
  the left, a fading scarlet sun

scorching pink the whole night air

the right,
a cool, calm stoic blue

driving through the middle
the whole sky feels like you

Hollie McNish

The Sky is Too Wide for Two Birds to Collide

Oi, sky, I have a question.
What is it like flossing pigeons out your teeth?
Why are you everywhere for no reason?
    What's it like to be nothing but a face?
Did you and the ocean ever swap positions
     so that it made more sense when it rained?

Sky, I have a request
since you have so much face
would you tattoo my dead friend under your eye?
You know the devil landed where I'm standing?
    You can put the sun back in your bag and call it off.

If earth does turn out to be flat, you reckon our egos will
  follow?
Aren't we nothing but a frisbee travelling towards some
  happy golden retriever?

Hey sky, we should compromise, say the earth is squashed
because that suggests you would be down here with us?
Me and my cousins could reach up,
itch that spot that's been bugging you for years.
That spot too wide for two birds to collide.

                       Kareem Parkins-Brown

There's a Person Reflected on the TV Calling their Dad

The seagulls are circling calling their dads,
the rain is calling its dad and so is the sun
and what's left of the lawn, a skyscraper
is kneeling and calling its dad, a bus, a train,
a city is calling its dad, the mouth
of an underground station opening, Halloween
has called, Christmas will call soon enough
and that new year climbing over the back wall
through the screen door is, of course,
calling its dad. I stand in a room and call my dad,
tell his answer machine not to worry anymore,
that they have found his body.

Joe Carrick-Varty

For a Father

Remember after work you grabbed our skateboard,
crouched like a surfer, wingtips over the edge;
wheels clacketing down the pocked macadam,
you veered almost straight into the neighbor's hedge?
We ran after you laughing, shouting, Wait!

Or that August night you swept us to the fair?
The tallest person boarding the Ferris wheel,
you rocked our car right when we hit the apex
above the winking midway, to make us squeal.
Next we raced you to the games, shouting, Wait!

At your funeral, relatives and neighbors,
shaking our hands, said, "So young to have died!"
But we've dreamt you're just skating streets away,
striding the fairgrounds toward a wilder ride.
And we're still straggling behind, shouting, *Wait—!*

Elise Partridge

Congratulations

for getting on with it all –
for eating cake and doing sums
at the table your dad's body lay on.
For making tea and choosing funeral shoes,
for just taking it all in and only once
a couple of years on lying on the floor
to scream.

There should be stickers for these things.
There should be cards to say well done
for walking past three of your alternate endings
in the street without losing it,
without peeling *what-ifs* off the pavement
and stuffing them in your mouth to try to taste
looser spit.

Trophies should be awarded for replying politely
to pointless emails on the days you remember
what a dead body looks like –
on mornings when you wake and for a second
the dream is still real and your dad
is going to pop round later and fix that door
or at least try.

Erin Bolens

How to Say Goodbye

Go to the crematorium.
Pay your respects.
Share fond memories.
Listen to the fond memories
of others.
Give and accept hugs.
Accept there is no right thing
to say at a time like this.
Accept whatever you feel
at any given moment.
Numb. Angry. Fucking angry.
Fucking furious.
Cry at any given moment.
Your tears are never inappropriate,
never too much,
never embarrassing.
Though it may feel this way,
you will not flood the world
with your grief if you let it out.
You may well drown yourself
if you hold it in.
Hold on to what his life meant.
Drink in his memory.
Drink to his memory.
Drink because you need a drink.

Drink some more,
even though you know you shouldn't.
Pour libations to him
on the carpet of a Wetherspoons.
Talk about him to people
who never even knew him, whenever
and for as long as you need.
Do not be afraid to say
the word suicide:
hold the word out like a serpent
you have tamed,
allow those with trembling hands
to touch the smooth scales
on the lower end of its long body
while you keep a firm grip
on its head.
Look the serpent in the eyes
as its tongue flickers.
Unwrap and release yourself.
Place it on the ground
and let it slip away.
It is not yours.
Make a promise
to be a friend to yourself.
Know when you need support.
If you ever feel your own serpent
creeping up your arm,
call someone with a steady hand
and a firm grip.
Be honest enough to admit

your grief is mostly about you.
Do not feel guilty when
something makes you smile,
laugh or excites you so much
that you momentarily forget
that pain and sorrow exist
in the world, let alone within you.
These are the moments you live for.
These are the moments
that have kept you alive.
Realise there is so much
more grief ahead
but hopefully enough
moments worth living for.
Remember,
none of us can make it out alive.
My friend.
There is no wrong way to die.
And there is no right way
to say goodbye.

Dean Atta

What the Living Do

Johnny, the kitchen sink has been clogged for days, some
   utensil probably
         fell down there.

And the Drano won't work but smells dangerous, and the
   crusty dishes
         have piled up

waiting for the plumber I still haven't called. This is the
   everyday
         we spoke of.
It's winter again: the sky's a deep, headstrong blue, and
   the sunlight
         pours through

the open living-room windows because the heat's on too
   high in here and
         I can't turn it off.
For weeks now, driving, or dropping a bag of groceries in
   the street,
         the bag breaking,

I've been thinking: This is what the living do. And
   yesterday, hurrying
         along those
wobbly bricks in the Cambridge sidewalk, spilling my
   coffee down my

wrist and sleeve,

I thought it again, and again later, when buying a
hairbrush: This is it.
Parking. Slamming the car door shut in the cold. What you
called
that yearning.

What you finally gave up. We want the spring to come and
the winter to pass.
We want
whoever to call or not call, a letter, a kiss—we want more
and more and
then more of it.

But there are moments, walking, when I catch a glimpse of
myself in the
window glass,
say, the window of the corner video store, and I'm gripped
by a cherishing
so deep

for my own blowing hair, chapped face, and unbuttoned
coat that I'm
speechless:
I am living. I remember you.

Marie Howe

L'appel du Vide

Cuz, knife in hand. I cut the top off and score
a deep cross in the okra. Top down,
I begin slicing sideward through its body.
Watching its sticky seeds latch onto me,
like a new-borns grip to a finger.
Plaster in sight, I proceed to test, upping my pace.

My lady asks *what's wrong*? I say *nothing*.
I ask, *why?* She says that I have been grinding
my teeth again while sleeping.
That nudges to ribs do nothing to stop it.
At night she hears them - a seesaw,
weighing into each other.

The weight of a uniform and a stranger
flattened his lungs the same way I'd sit
to deflate a mattress. Nameless are
the boulders that rocked side to side
on named Rashan Charles, until becoming still.
Justice is an autopsy with no apology.

Okra on the stove to boil. I begin peeling
the mackerel. Thumbing through its glossed
skin - only half enters the pot.
Followed by a sprinkle of maggi,
and the satirised stirring of my mother.

The flames burst uninvited in the building,
Uprooting through sleep, late dinners and
bath time. Jolting droplets of water into skin.
Each sensor unable to detect smoke from flesh.
Toddlers darting downwards out of balconies
through the blackest sky, wondering
the whereabouts of their superheroes.

The night before last I woke, questioning what's
happening to the men in my life. Just yesterday,
the hypocrite in me dared to ask a client why
he holds his anger in. Yesterday, I longed
for a pull of lemon haze, then remembered
why I decided not to learn how to roll.

I called out a friend's attempt at banter online
last week /an onslaught of projections from myself
in his inbox. A trauma that cannot be wiped,
it felt good, it felt right, until his sorry shone
a reflection, until my lady chuckled at my seriousness.
It was meant to be funny, he said. I don't get white
humour I thought to reply, I'm sorry.

My son turns his back to me yet again when being told off.
He too has mastered society's way of silencing me.
Angered I turn him / forward facing, stern.
His eyes are closed. He too has mastered the art
of choosing what to see. A friend stops me to advise
He who is good with the hammer treats everything as if it
  is a nail.

A Roanoke nightmare in Virginia. Outside the church
they stood. Holding Tiki Torches chanting the plight
of their whiteness, still – the privilege in using what isn't
there's to fuel their anger. Earlier that day a Black
    policeman
is instructed to guard neo nazi campaigners from attack.
His mouth on a leash, his blood, an implosion of
    aneephya,
a waving of flags behind him.

My lady asks *what's wrong?* I say, *everything.*
I pour Garri into scolding water and stir gently.
It bubbles and pops like lava, landing on my
novice skin. Love is faint if my wrist does not
ache while forming its body. A slab of Eba, ila,
Omi Obe and Eran on a plate. My hand,
Cupping, blowing, and layering. My teeth,
grinding solids into nothings.

Yomi Ṣode

Chapter 5

When we are drunk in each other's skin, there is a softer light, a bashment tune sweat beads bringing hair back to full life

HIBAQ OSMAN

Tonight!

Come out with me tonight.
Come out tonight.
Come not just out
but out out,
for delicious hiding,
for best versions,
big moves, fast choices.

The night is crunchy inviting,
open for business,
constantly tilting,
enemy of dawn.

Come out tonight.
Let's climb down untethered drainpipes
let's swim in celebrated oceans
let's get admitted to literary hospitals
let's make out with Bauhaus waitresses
let's cross serendipitous bridges
let's drink milkshakes in graveyards.

The night is a smashed lamp,
an empty inbox
a harmless explosion
a flammable cactus
a baklava tower

an indigo dickhead
and it never ends

until it does.
Then, dawn insists.
Morning hits.
Ugh, morning.
That brutalist cruise ship
that perky entrepreneur
that confronting leotard
that demoralising saxophone
that naked seminar
that opportunity for growth.

I'd love to love daytime but
I'm mourning the starlight.
Please say you'll come out again, tonight?

Molly Naylor

Holy Roller

by rhythm by fire by force i'm sure
we moved wicked everything licking

    hungry

    sure we tasted something like umami
in the heat of it

how we wined we maybe whined
to it to sing a thing too honest too unruly
maybe singed

    when the day of pentecost come

we were one accord
one place   of this i'm sure

    it was a sunday
but of course   outside was a cold

that we mocked and that mocked
in turn   an ocean

on a bucket list that pagans swam in

i believing foolish in the heat of it
assumed sweat was communion
    fever god given

music   an undressing

the backdrop to a tonguing   and spirit
and spirit gave utterance and

spirit on all flesh
      and we were all filled
and we were

well done holy
      darkened swarthy bitter

as moon into blood become night

say darkening needed

      say we got the whine wrong
      forgot what we was whining for

Gboyega Odubanjo

Hip-Hop Ghazal

Gotta love us brown girls, munching on fat, swinging blue
  hips,
decked out in shells and splashes, Lawdie, bringing them
  woo hips.

As the jukebox teases, watch my sistas throat the
  heartbreak,
inhaling bassline, cracking backbone and singing thru
  hips.

Like something boneless, we glide silent, seeping 'tween
  floorboards,
wrapping around the hims, and *ooh wee*, clinging like glue
  hips.

Engines grinding, rotating, smokin', gotta pull back some.
Natural minds are lost at the mere sight of ringing true
  hips.

Gotta love us girls, just struttin' down Manhattan streets
killing the menfolk with a dose of that stinging view. Hips.

Crying 'bout getting old—Patricia, you need to get up off
what God gave you. Say a prayer and start slinging. Cue
  hips.

Patricia Smith

117

Glory Be to the Gang Gang Gang

In praise of all that is honest, call upon the acrylic tips
and make a minaret out of a middle finger, gold-dipped
and counting. In the name of Filet-O-Fish, pink lemonade,
the sweat on an upper lip, the backing swell and ache
of Abdul Basit Abdus Samad on cassette tape, a clean
   jump shot,
the fluff of Ashanti's sideburns, the rice left in the pot
the calling cards and long waits, the seasonal burst
of baqalah-bought dates.

Every time they leave and come back
alive.

Birthmarks shaped like border disputes.
Black sand. Shah Rukh's dimples, like bullets
taking our aunts back to those summer nights,
these blessings on blessings on blessings.

Give me the rub of calves,
rappers sampling jazz,
the char of frankincense
and everything else that makes sense
in a world that don't.

Momtaza Mehri

Acknowledgments

you save me half a bag of skins, the hard parts, my fav,
dusted orange with hot

·

you say we can't go to the bar cause you're taking your
braids out
i come over, we watch madea while we pull you from you

·

you make us tacos with the shells i like & you don't

·

i get too drunk at the party, you scoop my pizza from the
sink with a solo cup, all that red

·

you, in the morning, bong water grin, wet chin

·

you, in the lawless dark, laughing like a room of women
laugh
at a man who thinks his knowledge is knowledge

·

i text you & you say, *i was bout to text you, bitch*

•

you cook pork chops same way i do, our families in
another city go to the same church

•

you, rolling a blunt, holding your son, is a mecca

•

you invite me out for drag queens on the nights i think of
finally [ ]

•

you pull over in Mississippi so i can walk a road my
grandfather bled on

•

you gave me a stone turtle, it held your palm's scent for a
week

•

i call your mama mama

•

you request like a demand, *make me some of that mango
cornbread*
i cut the fruit, measure the honey

•

you & you & you & you go in on a dildo for my birthday
you name it drake, you know me

•

a year with you in that dirty house with that cracked-out
cat was a good year

•

at the function, i feel myself splitting into too many rooms
of static
you touch my hand & there i am

•

do you want to be best friends?
a box for yes, a box for no

•

did our grandmothers flee the fields of embers so we
could find each other here?
friend, you are the war's gentle consequence

•

i am the prison that turns to rain in your hands

•

you, at my door the night my father leapt beyond what we
know
you, dirt where i plant my light

•

the branches of silence are heavy with your sweet seed

•

you smell like the milk of whatever beast i am

•

your poop is news, your fart is news, your gross body my
favorite song

•

you, drunk as an uncle, making all kinds of nonsense sense
i listen for the language between your words

•

& when we fight, not a ring, but a room with no exit
we spill the blood & bandage the wound, clean burns with
our tongues

•

if luck calls your name, we split the pot
& if you wither, surely i rot

•

we hate the same people, we say *nigga please* with the
same mouth

•

& before we were messy flesh, i'm sure we were the same dust

·

everywhere you are is a church, & i am the pastor, the deacons, the mothers fainting at the altar

·

as long as i am a fact to you, death can do with me what she wants

·

my body, water, your body, a trail of hands carrying the river to the sea

·

i ink your name into my arm to fasten what is already there

·

i would love you even if you killed god

·

you made coming out feel like coming in from the storm

·

you are the country i bloody the hills for

·

you love me despite the history of my hands, their
mangled confession

.

at the end of the world, let there be you, my world

.

god bless you who screens all my nudes, drafts my break-
up text

.

you are the drug that knocks the birds from my heart

.

ain't no mountain, no valley, no river i wouldn't give the
hands for comin' to you sideways

.

o the horrid friends who were just ships harboring me to
you

.

& how many times have you loved me without my
asking?
how often have i loved a thing because you loved it?
including me

& i always knew

•

with yo ugly ass

Danez Smith

Angel Nafis

The Birds

My friend bleeds on the picnic blanket.
She reaches down, expecting the damp
of a spilt tinny but feels warm, sees red.

We flock to cover her stained summer
dress, magicians releasing doves
from our pockets; tissues, make-up
wipes, a sanitary pad. We waddle,
a gaggle, to the park bogs.

From the sky perhaps we are one
bird, the drunkest a beak squawking,
two of us for wings, two for tail feathers
and her, the bleeding beating heart.

Laurie Ogden

A Poem in which I Try to Express My Glee at the Music My Friend Has Given Me

—for Patrick Rosal

Because I must not
get up to throw down in a café in the Midwest,
I hold something like a clownfaced herd
of bareback and winged elephants
stomping in my chest,
I hold a thousand
kites in a field loosed from their tethers
at once, I feel
my skeleton losing track
somewhat of the science I've made of tamp,
feel it rising up shriek and groove,
rising up a river guzzling a monsoon,
not to mention the butterflies
of the loins, the hummingbirds
of the loins, the thousand
dromedaries of the loins, oh body
of sunburst, body
of larkspur and honeysuckle and honeysuccor
bloom, body of treetop holler,
oh lightspeed body
of gasp and systole, the mandible's ramble,

the clavicle swoon, the spine's
trillion teeth oh, drift
of hip oh, trill of ribs,
oh synaptic clamor and juggernaut
swell oh gutracket
blastoff and sugartongue
syntax oh throb and pulse and rivulet
swing and glottal thing
and kick-start heart and heel-toe heart
ooh ooh ooh a bullfight
where the bull might
take flight and win!

Ross Gay

Soup Sister

And, of course,
it bothers me greatly that I can't know
the quality of the light where you are.
How your each day pans out,
how the breeze lifts the dry leaves from the street
or how the street pulls away from the rain.

Last week I passed a tree
that was exactly you in tree form,
with a kind look and tiny sub-branches
like your delicate wrists.

Six years ago we were lying
in a dark front room on perpendicular sofas,
so hungover that our skin hurt to touch.
How did we always manage
to be heartbroken at the same time?

I could chop, de-seed and roast
a butternut squash for dinner
in the time it took you to shower.

Steam curtained the windows, whiting out
the rain, which hit the house sideways.
One of us, though I forget who, said
do you think women are treated like bowls
waiting to be filled with soup?

And the other one said, of course.

Now the world is too big,
and it's sinking and rising
and stretching out its back bones.

The rivers are too wild,
the mountains are so so old
and it's all laid out arrogantly between us.

My friend, how long do you stand
staring at the socks in your drawer
lined up neat as buns in a bakery,
losing track of time and your place in the world,
in the (custardy light of a) morning?

Rebecca Perry

A Weekend of Life Drawing

I have seen my friends naked

Not enough space for time or secrecy,
one has scars that print her body
It feels like looking in a mirror

Another bares all and chit-chats,
Through various stages of dressing,
undressing, redressing

When we are drunk in each other's skin,
there is a softer light, a bashment tune
sweat beads bringing hair back to full life

We do not count each other's limbs
always close enough to hold hands,
cup watering faces just to say

you are the most beautiful thing I have ever known

I have seen my friends lonely,
seen them levitate whilst walking

Hibaq Osman

Chapter 6

I can't remember the tale,
but hear his voice still,
a well of dark water, a
prayer.

LI-YOUNG LEE

Heirlooms

The stein with a chipped edge
you're sure you bought for a quid
on Camden High St. belonged,
if you ask me, as well you might,
to my mother, known all her life
by a name she detested.

What does it mean
to answer to a misnomer
to feel the cold air
between being and being seen?

We have filled
our house with her things:
Alfred Meakin Dinner Set,
cutlery etched with the indicia
of the Newcastle Corporation,
made in Sheffield by Firth Steelworks,
a white drop leaf, crystalline glassware,
a house-proud woman's cache.

I live in an artist's impression
of the flat in Wandsworth.
I cut vegetables with the knife
my mother reached for in her rage
I remember the sound
of metal scraping wood;

the door
I had just grown strong
enough to hold closed.

Kayo Chingonyi

Dowry

The tablecloth was crocheted by
my mother's mother's mother's mother
in a plump lavender field,
in a long-forgotten
Europe between the wars.
'My dowry'

Safta left a coffee ring on it.
I remember it on the sideboard,
spread under a cigarette display case.
From my nan I inherited
a tin of peaches and
a tin of custard.

They were still in date a year after
she died, I was going to make a trifle
on her birthday but found that dad
had eaten the syrupy fruit on a night
when he missed his mum,
spooning the juice like an airplane.

Talia Randall

AMAI VAKO

iv   dzivaresekwa 3

You learnt to sing from your mother
who often sang for herself.

You were a shadow   a dark corner,
curls of smoke rising from your face.

                    In the song
you only knew how to shudder
in that thin space between brain & blood
                    dream & lucidity.

There's a recurring dream, family rumour
that you were born with gills
                    liquefied by your first cry –
turning a fish baby like you into a girl child.

MwanaSikana akarega kushambira;
kaupenyu kanenge motokari-fi.

BabyGirl   who gave up swimming
approached life as a parked car
                    still & switched off.

Inherited her father's sins, a life of chasing
East to West when home is really South,
where the music punctuates milestones.

You learnt to sing from your mother
way before the day she said
enough is enough & left.
                    Her side of the wardrobe empty
save for the cotton top   silk bottom
white dress your Baba bought her
on the day you were born

weeks late   clinging to life
protected by water.

v **mazowe** *(1990)*

Remember
your *amai* once was a girl too,
adolescent,
a curious young being,
with skin like salted caramel
& a mouth
full of salt, lemon, all things unsweet,
your *amai*
was once a girl too.
Who, like you, knew
how to squander a whole night's sleep
on fantasy,
to swap it for full days of broad, deep slumber
through heartbreak,
through the last sliver
of dim light, falling through the blinds
soon after sunset.

She would tell you
how hairless your head was,
stuck between her thighs
for hours. How the midwife told her
swallow, breathe
before asking if her father's sisters
hadn't taught her that real, strong
women birthed in silence,
tongues tucked
behind gritted teeth.

The times she used belts,
switches, extension cords
for broken cups, curfew slips
& other small things.
You cried for her, mostly for yourself,
could never tell from those red welts
if it was that you looked like your father
or because
                    birthing you almost killed her.

Belinda Zhawi

Twenty Five

There's a Thai Food Gourmet on Horseferry Road. The walls inside are painted a warm yellow, bars tables and seats are wooden trimmed with gold. It's a place for parties: from benefits to birthdays gatherings, where such important dates are sown. Today we've claimed it made it our own. The walls are not yellow, they are sun-painted stained windows, the wood is improvised from forests where the fauna roam free, untainted. To celebrate a wedding anniversary, collected here are family members and close friends, those that'll stick together till forever ends /

    The couple have been paired for twenty-five years. They know the square root of survival, how to float four children through tidal waves to safe piers. My mother is the most magnificent woman in the world, my father's words are final. His voice (an older model of mine) rises above the conjugal ensemble. He says *there are secrets to a marriage like this. Number one, the wife is always right, especially when she is wrong. Number two on the list, never let a dispute last over a day long.* He plays the part, choir-master to the chorus-like laughter of these friends in sun-rays /

    In the silence after, my father thanks God for we four kids, pride bursting, in a louder tone – growing – says he'd be nothing without mother at his side. My mother

hugs him, her face bright, soft, and there is a passion here,
a vintage love, refined as a twenty-five year old battle-
dove, body battered but stronger and sublime. I've seen
beginnings of passion like this, in faces of girlfriends, in the
slowed-down times. It suddenly strikes me: mother was
once a girl; all short skirts and madness, a thing without a
care, nothing but the Nigerian night in her hair /

The speech ends to applause and own devices. We quaff
champagne, scoff cake slices. I am eating and listening
as the babble rises when Rachel (sister's friend) tells me
a curious thing, of a boy she gets on with; they're like
fuel and fire - with them, it's almost always all flames,
sapphire-furnace cuddles and ridiculous love names, says
for a thing beyond her power the man is just a friend. The
reason dowses fire, tames to an end, says he is from the
same tribe as she is – back home, it is against tradition,
it's a strict taboo for same tribe members to be as lovers
should /

Neither of them dare to break the age-old custom.
Surprised such a rule crossed oceans, climbed time,
found these two birds and cost them their wings, I want
to urge her to deny her tribe, instead, sit silenced by the
sadness in her sighs. Sweeping across the tables, I see
the reason why - My parents, similar customs, twenty-five
years joined. Whilst such rules are ancient it has kept them
strong, in truth, there are two sides to every coin. What
demand holds this on future love?

Scanning the numbers for my little sister, finds all three by the Karaoke machine. Picture this: the youngest between the older other two / hands on hips / heads swing side-to-side / thrown back / lost in the spiritual sing of a tri-vocal harmonious band… They are wailing to Michael Jackson's Smooth Criminal *Annie are you okay / are you okay / are you okay Annie? /*

The moment is a monument to richness. Uncle laughs, thanks God they are in school *you'd never make it in the music business.* My sisters are spectacular (in that single-mothers-are -super-heroes sort of way), whatever future love feigns, let it come, for Mum became a little girl again and my sisters have super powers. We knowers of the way, we wave riders will find safe bays again. So Michael, on this most glorious of days, believe it, Annie is fine, Annie is okay /

Inua Ellams

142

The Little Miracles

After 'A Winter Night' by Tomas Tranströmer
(translated by Robin Roberston)

Since I found mother collapsed on the kitchen
floor, we siblings have become blindfolded mules

harnessed to carts filled with strain, lumbering
through a relentless storm, wanting to make

our mother walk on her own again, wanting to rest
our palms on her left leg and arm like Jesus, but

constellations do not gather like leaves in a teacup,
so what miracle, of what blood, of what feeble wishes

do we pray, happy no nails hammer plywood, building
a coffin, to house her dead weight, happy her journey

crawls as we her children hold on like drought holds out
for rain, learning what it is like to begin again, start

with the, the, the dog, the cat, the date, the year, the
stroke, the brain, the fenced in walls, she struggles

to dismantle brick on brick. *She cannot break this,*
we reason, watching her left hand in her lap, a useless

echo. We chew bitter bush, swallow our howling storm,
reluctantly splintering under the strain of our mother's

ailing bed-rest. We smile at each of her feats: right hand
brushing her teeth in late evening, head able to lift

without the aid of a neck-brace, her off spring's names
Malika, Phillip and Kwesi are chants repeated over

and over as if staking us children as her life's work,
her blessings, showing how much we are loved. The days

she sings *walk with me oh my Lord,* over and over, *walk
with me oh my Lord, through the darkest night…* and I
   sing

with her, my tones flat to her soprano, *just as you changed
the wind and walked upon the sea, conquer, my living
   Lord,*

the storm that threatens me, and we sing and sing until
she says, *Maliks, please stop the cat-wailing before*

*you voice mek rain fall, and look how the weather nice
outside eh!* Then we laugh and laugh until almost giddy,

our mood light momentarily in this sterile room, where
each spoonful of pureed food slipped into her mouth

like a tender offering takes us a step away from feeding
tubes, and we are so thankful for each minuscule miracle.

                                                          Malika Booker

Sing To Me and Do Not Die of Thirst

Alzheimer's patients sing every lyric to their favourite
  songs,
and this casual act becomes a dance with defiance.
Research shows our memory of music remains intact,
like the clothes of a missing child kept by a mother;
the brain stores music in a different place,
  —a subtle precaution.

My grandmother bathes my grandfather
and lyrics spill from his mouth
like water from a drowned child.
He sings Johnny Nash's 'I Can See Clearly Now'
in a bass so sharp it cuts the water in half
to form a space my grandmother can walk through.
He saw water: his brain's automatic response was
to regurgitate a song that had the word 'rain' in it.
My grandmother takes in his voice
  and her skin splits open like an overstuffed suitcase.
My God, it must hurt for someone you love
to remember a song in clearer detail than your face.

She wonders how he knows to accentuate *blue ska-yeee-*
  aies.
Proof that music muscle memory
can stretch more than shaki meat.

My grandmother joins in to harmonise,
the Bible says two shall become one voice and live till
death cracks the voice in half; I paraphrased out of anger.
Her voice is shaky as waist beads on a Fela Kuti back-up
   dancer,
grief tugs on your vocal chords like heavy braids,
leaves it with sore and thinning edges.

As they harmonise my grandmother morphs into the song,
wipes water from her husband's face, sings
I can see clearly now the rain is gone,
and once again they are two vivacious youths
whirling though a garden in summer.
He says "you look like the girl Mona I danced with"
and the water in the bathtub levitates to become rain.

Theresa Lola

Ruins

Here's my body
in the bath, all the skin's
inflamed trenches
and lost dominions,

my belly's fallen keystone
its slackened tilt –
for all the Aztec gold
I'd not give up

this room where you slept,
your spine to my right,
your head
stoppered in my pelvis

like a good amen –
amen I say
to my own damn bulk,
my milk-stretched breasts –

amen I say to all of this
if I have you –
your screw-ball smile
at every dawn,

your half-pitched, milk-wild smile
at every waking call,
my loved-beyond-all-reason
darling, dark-eyed girl.

Fiona Benson

biriyani

waking up is waking up yesterday is waking up the day
before and getting my mum on the phone to tell her I love
her but settling for saying I miss her biriyani. The other
day I wept at a romcom, it wasn't the romcom I wept for
but the thought of my mum not being there to tell me
she found an article in The Guardian she thought I'd like,
kept it in an envelope marked with my name, when I was
a child I'd wait for everyone to go out before trying on her
clothes, stuffing her bra with my socks, bumbling around
the kitchen table pretending to serve dinner. Today I watch
my mother reading the Sunday papers, her face setting
into folds, specs balancing like a youngster on the edge
of a bridge. I blink so as to catch it, imagine I am a camera
and my mother is developing on the inside of my eyelid.

Arji Manelpillai

Chick

We talked about you all the time.
Dan said he saw you ironing cellophane.
I said you'd let me hold a thousand pounds.
We found a hollow-soled shoe.

My cousins loved your tricks.
They'd follow the lady, search your sleeves,
blow luck into your fist. Mum called you a croupier.
At school I said you drove a cab.

Most days you were back at dawn.
I watched through a crack as you slept,
a hump of blankets in the purple light,
the smell of sweat.

I saw you once Dad, knelt over cards,
strewn on the floor, panic on your face.
For God's sake, Chick, you said
You couldn't do the marks.

Then, each Tuesday, £16.30 – a paper,
tobacco, one hand of Kalooki. You sunk
into the settee like you'd been kicked there,
shouted in the bathroom, asked me for money.

At the wake, a ring of phlegmy men
with yellow eyes and meaty skin, told me

what your name meant, placed the ace of hearts
across your coffin, flowers shaped as dice.

Hannah Lowe

Happy Birthday Moon

Dad reads aloud. I follow his finger across the page.
sometimes his finger moves past words, tracing white
   space.
He makes the Moon say something new every night
to his deaf son who slurs his speech.

Sometimes his finger moves past words, tracing white
   space.
Tonight he gives the Moon my name, but I can't say it,
his deaf son who slurs his speech.
Dad taps the page, says, *try again.*

Tonight he gives the Moon my name, but I can't say it.
I say *Rain-an Akabok*. He laughs.
Dad taps the page, says, try again,
but I like making him laugh. I say my mistake again.

I say *Rain-an Akabok*. He laughs,
says, *Raymond you're something else*.
I like making him laugh. I say my mistake again.
Rain-an Akabok. What else will help us?

He says, *Raymond you're something else*.
I'd like to be the Moon, the bear, even the rain.
Rain-an Akabok, what else will help us
hear each other, really hear each other?

I'd like to be the Moon, the bear, even the rain.
Dad makes the Moon say something new every night
and we hear each other, really hear each other.
As Dad reads aloud, I follow his finger across the page.

Raymond Antrobus

The Gift

To pull the metal splinter from my palm
my father recited a story in a low voice.
I watched his lovely face and not the blade.
Before the story ended, he'd removed
the iron sliver I thought I'd die from.

I can't remember the tale,
but hear his voice still, a well
of dark water, a prayer.
And I recall his hands,
two measures of tenderness
he laid against my face,
the flames of discipline
he raised above my head.

Had you entered that afternoon
you would have thought you saw a man
planting something in a boy's palm,
a silver tear, a tiny flame.
Had you followed that boy
you would have arrived here,
where I bend over my wife's right hand.

Look how I shave her thumbnail down
so carefully she feels no pain.
Watch as I lift the splinter out.
I was seven when my father

took my hand like this,
and I did not hold that shard
between my fingers and think,
Metal that will bury me,
christen it Little Assassin,
Ore Going Deep for My Heart.
And I did not lift up my wound and cry,
Death visited here!
I did what a child does
when he's given something to keep.
I kissed my father.

Li-Young Lee

I Hope You Stopped for the Swans

It's hard to recognise longing
filling up the body like a rock pool.
Looking behind me at the wall,
why it is always four O' clock?

I hear knocking when I'm sleeping,
but I don't see your face anymore.
Come inside, shake the water off my love,
you've had a skinfull.

Somewhere our dad is on a hill
with his waterproof map. He'll send me
a long text later about being at London Bridge,
eating a Cornish pasty.

I'll reply, 'Renationalise the railways!'
by which I mean, I love you
and I am sorry your son died.
How we used to beg him to bury us in the sand.

There are small mercies; my soft father.
I don't think about him crumbling apart
on the kitchen stool,
how seven minutes later he was back to normal,

singing under his breath, spreading apricot jam.
The sky is thin today
like a torn off blister
and he is underneath it, walking.

Cecilia Knapp

Full-Time Driver

I took every hour they offered, delivering
lukewarm pizzas by means of an '86
LeSabre, the back tires almost bald.
Managers rarely yelled or wore me out
about moving too slow. When we blundered
orders, most customers understood.
My brother worked there too. He was beautiful.
I should've kissed him, one good forehead kiss
while such a gesture might've mattered.
Women, shoeless in their doorways, gave me
resigned smiles as they paid. Undergraduate
smokers proposed hits of their burning herb.
The richest part was when business
would ebb, and I'd coast the summer streets.
The air felt like a cool fruit. The engine block
churned a sure tune. The rearview caught
moments of low moons. Time was a tame lake
my hand skimmed from the front of a canoe.

Marcus Jackson

William

at four days old

When the lock chucks familiar,
or a cat follows its name from a room,
when silence is strung, or rain
holds back the trees, I thought
I had the lever of these.
But weighing your fine melon head,
your innocent daring to be,
and mouth-first searching,
your tiny fist is allowed absolutely
and I am uncooked
– I can feel my socks being on –
utter, precious apple,
churchyards flatten in my heart,
I've never been so brilliant so scared.

Jack Underwood

Here

Here I am in the garden laughing
an old woman with heavy breasts
and a nicely mapped face

how did this happen
well that's who I wanted to be

at last a woman
in the old style sitting
stout thighs apart under
a big skirt grandchild sliding
on off my lap a pleasant
summer perspiration

that's my old man across the yard
he's talking to the meter reader
he's telling him the world's sad story
how electricity is oil or uranium
and so forth I tell my grandson
run over to your grandpa ask him
to sit beside me for a minute I
am suddenly exhausted by my desire
to kiss his sweet explaining lips.

Grace Paley

Chapter 7

listen I love you joy is coming

KIM ADDONIZIO

What Seems Like Joy

how much history is enough history   before we can agree
to flee our daycares   to wash everything away and start
   over
leaving laptops to be lost in the wet along with housecats
   and
              Christ's
own mother   even a lobster climbs away from its shell a
   few
times a life   but every time I open my eyes I find
I am still inside myself   each epiphany dull and familiar
oh now I am barefoot   oh now I am lighting the wrong
   end
of a cigarette   I just want to be shaken new like a flag
   whipping
away its dust   want to pull out each of my teeth
and replace them with jewels   I'm told what seems like
   joy
is often joy   that the soul lives in the throat plinking
like a copper bell   I've been so young for so many years
it's all starting to jumble together   joy jeweling
   copper   its plink   a throat   sometimes I feel beautiful
   and near dying
like a feather on an arrow shot through a neck   other
   times

I feel tasked only with my own soreness   like a scab on
   the roof
of a mouth   my father believed in gardens   delighting
at burying each thing in its potential for growth   some
   years
the soil was so hard the water seeped down slower than
   the green
seeped up   still he'd say *if you're not happy in your own
   yard*
you won't be happy anywhere   I've never had a yard but
   I've had
               apartments
where water pipes burst above my head   where I've
   scrubbed
a lover's blood from the kitchen tile   such cleaning
takes so much time you expect there to be confetti at the
   end
what we'll need in the next life   toothpaste   party hats
and animal bones   every day people charge out of this
   world
squealing   good-bye human behavior!   so long acres
of germless chrome!   it seems gaudy for them to be so
   cavalier
with their bliss   while I'm still here lurching into my labor
hanging by my hair from the roof of a chapel   churchlight
               thickening

around me   or wandering into the woods to pull apart
eggshells   emptying
them in the dirt   then sewing them back together to dry
   in the
               sun

Kaveh Akbar

Joy is Coming

If the front seat on the top deck is free, you take it. When you leave shops you don't say *goodbye* to the cashier anymore, you say *see you soon*. People are patient and you're learning to be patient. When singing songs from bad musicals you laugh with your mouth wide open. It doesn't make you cry because this time you deserve it. In a pub, your friends talk about drinking whilst drinking and you don't find an excuse to leave the table. You do at least one important thing a day without flinching. A kid who wants nothing else but for you to read their poem says *you know what, Miss, you're one of the good ones.* It's so great that you wish it was appropriate to put it on your fridge.

Emily Harrison

Not Even This

Hey.

I used to be a fag now I'm a checkbox.

The pen tip jabbed in my back, I feel the mark of progress.

I will not dance alone in the municipal graveyard at
    midnight, blasting sad
songs on my phone, for nothing.

I promise you, I was here. I felt things that made death so
    large it was
indistinguishable from air—and I went on destroying
    inside it like wind in
a storm.

The way Lil Peep says *I'll be back in the mornin'* when you
    know how it ends.

The way I kept dancing when the song was over, because
    it freed me.

The way the streetlight blinks once, before waking up for
    its night shift, like
we do.

The way we look up and whisper *sorry* to each other, the
    boy and I, when
there's teeth.

When there's always teeth, on purpose.

When I threw myself into gravity and made it work. Ha.

I made it out by the skin of my griefs.

I used to be a fag now I'm lit. Ha.

Once, at a party set on a rooftop in Brooklyn for an "artsy
    vibe," a young
woman said, sipping her drink, *You're so lucky. You're gay
    plus you get to*
write about war and stuff. I'm just white. [Pause.] *I got
    nothing.* [Laughter,
glasses clinking.]

Unlike feelings, blood gets realer when you feel it.

Because everyone knows yellow pain, pressed into
    American letters, turns
to gold.

Our sorrow Midas-touched. Napalm with a rainbow
    afterglow.

I'm trying to be real but it costs too much.

They say the Earth spins and that's why we fall but
    everyone knows it's the
music.

It's been proven difficult to dance to machine gun fire.

Still, my people made a rhythm this way. A way.

My people, so still, in the photographs, as corpses.

My failure was that I got used to it. I looked at us, mangled
    under the *TIME*
photographer's shadow, and stopped thinking, *Get up, get
    up.*

I saw the graveyard steam in the pinkish dawn and knew
    the dead were still
breathing. Ha.

If they come for me, take me home take me out.

What if it wasn't the crash that made me, but the debris?

What if it was meant this way: the mother, the lexicon, the
    line of cocaine on
the mohawked boy's collarbone in an East Village sublet in
    2007?

What's wrong with me, Doc? There must be a pill for this.

Too late—these words already shrapnel in your brain.

Impossible in high school, I am now the ultimate
    linebacker. I plow through
the page, making a path for you, dear reader, going
    nowhere.

Because the fairy tales were right. You'll need magic to
    make it out of here.

Long ago, in another life, on an Amtrak through Iowa, I
    saw, for a few blurred
seconds, a man standing in the middle of a field of winter
    grass, hands at his

side, back to me, all of him stopped there save for his hair
    scraped by low
wind.

When the countryside resumed its wash of gray wheat,
    tractors, gutted
barns, black sycamores in herdless pastures, I started to
    cry. I put my copy
of Didion's *The White Album* down and folded a new dark
    around my head.

The woman beside me stroked my back saying, in a
    Midwestern accent that
wobbled with tenderness, *Go on son. You get that out*
    now. No shame in
breakin' open. You get that out and I'll fetch us some
    tea. Which made me
lose it even more.

She came back with Lipton in paper cups, her eyes
    nowhere blue and there.
She was silent all the way to Missoula, where she got off
    and said, patting my
knee, *God is good. God is good.*

I can say it was beautiful now, my harm, because it
    belonged to no one else.

To be a dam for damage. My shittiness will not enter the
    world, I thought,
and quickly became my own hero.

Do you know how many hours I've wasted watching
    straight boys play video
games?

Enough.

Time is a mother.

Lest we forget, a morgue is also a community center.

In my language, the one I recall now only by closing my
    eyes, the word for
love is Yêu.

And the word for weakness is Yếu.

How you say what you mean changes what you say.

Some call this prayer. I call it watch your mouth.

When they zipped my mother in a body bag I
    whispered: Rose, get out of there.
Your plants are dying.

Enough is enough.

Body, doorway that you are, be more than what I'll pass
    through.

Stillness. That's what it was.

The man in the field in the red sweater, he was so still he
    became, somehow,
more true, like a knife wound in a landscape painting.

Like him, I caved.

I caved and decided it will be joy from now on. Then
   everything opened. The
lights blazed around me into a white weather

and I was lifted, wet and bloody, out of my mother,
   screaming

and enough.

                                          Ocean Vuong

Moments of Being

'Illness is the great confessional.'
Virginia Woolf, *On Being Ill.*

I went to hell and back and now I lie
recumbent in cotton in the privilege
of one convalescing from war

when friends ask I refer to myself only
as soldier as if
this battle were literal I no pacifist

healing is ugly magic only fools say different
LOVE and DEATH remain pinnacles for majors
I endure that blasted scrubland wild fabled
a complicated angel fails to locate a vein

I can handle censure but not sympathy
the crestfallen art of my troubled mother's
face how a voice trails off
changes octave Deepest Sympathies
Sorry I will die of love

quite happy but I get ahead of myself
I was discreet once I warranted cardboard
now I am seen in a mask I espoused on
the virtues of prioritised clenching a fist
pliant I was a damp sock regularly
frequented I would smile after annoyed

no one stayed longer so disavowed
community I am in need of
WHO and WHY bad talismans

I looked up at the sky saw only sky
willing an omen some petty harbinger – there
was only my mind-my body bereft of men
but choices arranged freakish human-sized
dolls sexless yes but all so orderly so monstrous

in health we maintain what is licensed the ill
remain what they are a problem until they are not
instead I seek the quiet dignity of plants Mugwort
is one I am fond of as one is fond of ugly daughters
their freedom but first I must consult womenfolk
down the telephone break eggs over saltwater
apply olive oil to lift curses from this body I return
to old beliefs certainties within thoroughly done
with *discourse*

BED is one such structure I have been lessoned in
I do not deconstruct a good nun prostrate
before matinee idol pillowcase saint-like sub
missive written neatly in the margins of vanishing

one morning I forget
I discover light
am genuinely offended

the stillness of carpets is terrible their unrelenting
momentum   The Sun   O   it's midday
sashay across the page a mawkish ancestor

blazing I am inert yet words hold
meaning I am no nihilist I know things

beneath
the wound another surface is
ripe for examining

I am sad but god willing
one sleight of hand ought to do it
I know tricks spirits I can muster
a PG ghost popular with children
friendly that is to say see through
cartoonish threat herein
attached I am terribly
to this life unfinished business
the rest of my existence

Oakley Flanagan

Giraffe

When you feel better from this — and you will — it will
be quiet and unremarkable, like walking into the next
room. It might sting a little, like warmth leaking into cold-
numbed hands. When you feel better, it will be the slow
clearing of static from the radio. It will be a film set when
the director yells *cut!* When you feel better, you will take:
a plastic spoon for your coffee foam, free chocolates from
the gleaming oak reception desk, the bus on sunny days,
your own sweet time. When you feel better, it will be like
walking barefoot on cool, smooth planks of wood, still
damp from last night's rain. It will be the holy silence when
the tap stops dripping. The moment a map finally starts
to make sense. When you feel better, you will still suffer,
but your sadness will be graspable, roadworthy, have
handlebars. When you feel better, you will not always be
happy, but when happiness does come, it will be long-
legged, sun-dappled: a giraffe.

Bryony Littlefair

City

I feel safest when walking
alone at night
I like it when the slices of a city start to make sense
when your body begins
to belong to the tune
of footsteps on pavement
when you change without realising

it's good to change
I never felt safe before
I felt I might rip through myself
as though the things I thought
and felt
but never said
were filling an overflowing vat
which would corrode or burst
and all of me would come rushing out

I had a lover who died from too much of himself I had a
friend who died from not enough
I'm a person I never thought I'd be
and that person
is quiet, tired
but tough

I found a home in a city outside me I found a home in a
silence within

I have a song
I'll never learn to sing but it's okay
I'll just keep on walking

Malaika Kegode

The Window

after Marie Howe

Once in a lifetime, you will gesture
at an open window, tell the one who
detests the queerness in you that *dead
daughters do not disappoint*, free your
sore knees from inching towards a kind
of reprieve, declare yourself genderless
as hawk or sparrow: an encumbered body
let loose from its cage. You will refuse your

mother's rage, her spit, her tongue heavy
like the heaviest of stones. Your mother's

anger is like the sun, which is like love,
which is the easiest thing – even on the

hardest of days. You will linger, knowing
that this standing before an open window

is what the living do, that they sometimes
reconsider at the slightest touch of grace.

Mary Jean Chan

To the Woman Crying Uncontrollably in the Next Stall

If you ever woke in your dress at 4am ever
closed your legs to a man you loved opened
them for one you didn't moved against
a pillow in the dark stood miserably on a beach
seaweed clinging to your ankles paid
good money for a bad haircut backed away
from a mirror that wanted to kill you bled
into the back seat for lack of a tampon
if you swam across a river under rain sang
using a dildo for a microphone stayed up
to watch the moon eat the sun entire
ripped out the stitches in your heart
because why not if you think nothing &
no one can / listen I love you joy is coming

Kim Addonizio

Inside.

Day breaks
at a pace that makes the face ache
and just for his faiths sake
he tries to stay calm
he looks down at his young mans hands and at his arms
and remembers a time
they seemed so much smaller
outside its grey and as the rain beats a rhythm on the
window pane
inside feels just the same
he remembers the game he used to play
at home on his own
racing the rain drops to the edge of the glass
back then he only had to ask
any questions
was always someone inside who seemed to have the
answers
in that house
that smelt of fresh pumpkin
fried dumpling, beans and Saturday cartoons
old tunes, Lee Perry and James Brown
when Soul II Soul came round he was rocking a fade
Super Mario got played and played
like the hand-me-down jungle tapes
his brother gave him from raves

everything was simple and nice
Granddad's advice
Nanna cookin peas and rice for ten children
cousins did the running man and whether it was sunny out
and hot or not
it never really mattered
first time he ever got battered by four kids
or on four quids worth of Tennent's Super
shared with James Cooper
both times he got the same feeling
that all he wanted to be
was back inside home
inside nothing could hurt him
the fortress
Castle Greyskull with mom as the Sorceress
of course
things changed
people died, people left, people lied
some turned strange
outside became home
two steps from fully grown
running with a crew, but in truth all alone
sitting in the park, hitting spliffs and getting high
not really fitting in
not really knowing why
different
only thing in common was boredom
keeping score of how many lips and trips they'd had
it went bad
the same old role play

picking up the dole pay and smoking to find home
inside and outside got blurred
so when he got hurt the only places to go
were the dark rooms
and now he's sitting in
going out less and less
smoking sess got in a mess internal voices
blames himself for bad choices
and with only himself to convince
it's a sinch to hear voices
no outside
inside became both
one minute haven
next second a nightmare
the whole world is right there
one third of an inch of that same glass is now too much to
ask
because it's grey on both sides
and nothing tastes worse in this world
than wasted time.
At this point the narrator steps up out of the paper
slaps his face to wake himself
it's now ten years later
days rolled like snow, avalanches of years
tears run off flushed cheeks and drown into beers
it appears that things change and people move on
but if you just squint your eyes, that perception is wrong
from inside to outside
it's nobody's choice
but what better way of getting out, than using my voice

from inside me to outside
inside you
from inside me to outside
inside
you

Steve Camden

At Last the New Arriving

Like the horn you played in Catholic school
the city will open its mouth and cry

out. *Don't worry 'bout nothing. Don't mean
no thing.* It will leave you stunned

as a fighter with his eyes swelled shut
who's told he won the whole damn purse.

It will feel better than any floor
that's risen up to meet you. It will rise

like Easter bread, golden and familiar
in your grandmother's hands. She'll come back,

heaven having been too far from home
to hold her. O it will be beautiful.

Every girl will ask you to dance and the boys
won't kill you for it. Shake your head.

Dance until your bones clatter. What a prize
you are. What a lucky sack of stars.

Gabrielle Calvocoressi

Instructions on Not Giving Up

More than the fuchsia funnels breaking out
of the crabapple tree, more than the neighbor's
almost obscene display of cherry limbs shoving
their cotton candy-colored blossoms to the slate
sky of Spring rains, it's the greening of the trees
that really gets to me. When all the shock of white
and taffy, the world's baubles and trinkets, leave
the pavement strewn with the confetti of aftermath,
the leaves come. Patient, plodding, a green skin
growing over whatever winter did to us, a return
to the strange idea of continuous living despite
the mess of us, the hurt, the empty. Fine then,
I'll take it, the tree seems to say, a new slick leaf
unfurling like a fist to an open palm, I'll take it all.

Ada Limón

Wind in a Box

—after Lorca
I want to always sleep beneath a bright red blanket
of leaves. I want to never wear a coat of ice.
I want to learn to walk without blinking.

I want to outlive the turtle and the turtle's father,
the stone. I want a mouth full of permissions

and a pink glistening bud. If the wildflower and ant hill
can return after sleeping each season, I want to walk
out of this house wearing nothing but wind.

I want to greet you, I want to wait for the bus with you
weighing less than a chill. I want to fight off the bolts

of gray lighting the alcoves and winding paths
of your hair. I want to fight off the damp nudgings
of snow. I want to fight off the wind.

I want to be the wind and I want to fight off the wind
with its sagging banner of isolation, its swinging

screen doors, its gilded boxes, and neatly folded
    pamphlets
of noise. I want to fight off the dull straight lines
of two by fours and endings, your disapprovals,

your doubts and regulations, your carbon copies.
If the locust can abandon its suit,

I want a brand new name. I want the pepper's fury
and the salt's tenderness. I want the virtue
of the evening rain, but not its gossip.

I want the moon's intuition, but not its questions.
I want the malice of nothing on earth. I want to enter

every room in a strange electrified city
and find you there. I want your lips around the bell of flesh

at the bottom of my ear. I want to be the mirror,
but not the nightstand. I do not want to be the light switch.
I do not want to be the yellow photograph

or book of poems. When I leave this body, Woman,
I want to be pure flame. I want to be your song.

Terrance Hayes

Everything is Going to be All Right

How should I not be glad to contemplate
the clouds clearing beyond the dormer window
and a high tide reflected on the ceiling?
There will be dying, there will be dying,
but there is no need to go into that.
The poems flow from the hand unbidden
and the hidden source is the watchful heart.
The sun rises in spite of everything
and the far cities are beautiful and bright.
I lie here in a riot of sunlight
watching the day break and the clouds flying.
Everything is going to be all right.

Derek Mahon

Wild Geese

You do not have to be good.
You do not have to walk on your knees
for a hundred miles through the desert repenting.
You only have to let the soft animal of your body
love what it loves.
Tell me about despair, yours, and I will tell you mine.
Meanwhile the world goes on.
Meanwhile the sun and the clear pebbles of the rain
are moving across the landscapes,
over the prairies and the deep trees,
the mountains and the rivers.
Meanwhile the wild geese, high in the clean blue air,
are heading home again.
Whoever you are, no matter how lonely,
the world offers itself to your imagination,
calls to you like the wild geese, harsh and exciting -
over and over announcing your place
in the family of things.

Mary Oliver

Love after Love

The time will come
when, with elation
you will greet yourself arriving
at your own door, in your own mirror
and each will smile at the other's welcome,

and say, sit here. Eat.
You will love again the stranger who was your self.
Give wine. Give bread. Give back your heart
to itself, to the stranger who has loved you

all your life, whom you ignored
for another, who knows you by heart.
Take down the love letters from the bookshelf,

the photographs, the desperate notes,
peel your own image from the mirror.
Sit. Feast on your life.

Derek Walcott

Still I Rise

You may write me down in history
With your bitter, twisted lies,
You may trod me in the very dirt
But still, like dust, I'll rise.

Does my sassiness upset you?
Why are you beset with gloom?
'Cause I walk like I've got oil wells
Pumping in my living room.

Just like moons and like suns,
With the certainty of tides,
Just like hopes springing high,
Still I'll rise.

Did you want to see me broken?
Bowed head and lowered eyes?
Shoulders falling down like teardrops,
Weakened by my soulful cries?

Does my haughtiness offend you?
Don't you take it awful hard
'Cause I laugh like I've got gold mines
Diggin' in my own backyard.

You may shoot me with your words,
You may cut me with your eyes,
You may kill me with your hatefulness,

But still, like air, I'll rise.

Does my sexiness upset you?
Does it come as a surprise
That I dance like I've got diamonds
At the meeting of my thighs?

Out of the huts of history's shame
I rise
Up from a past that's rooted in pain
I rise
I'm a black ocean, leaping and wide,
Welling and swelling I bear in the tide.

Leaving behind nights of terror and fear
I rise
Into a daybreak that's wondrously clear
I rise
Bringing the gifts that my ancestors gave,
I am the dream and the hope of the slave.
I rise
I rise
I rise.

Maya Angelou

Help us make the next generation of readers

We – both author and publisher – hope you enjoyed this book.
We believe that you can become a reader at any time in your life,
but we'd love your help to give the next generation a head start.

Did you know that 9 per cent of children don't have a book of their
own in their home, rising to 13 per cent in disadvantaged families*?
We'd like to try to change that by asking you to consider the role
you could play in helping to build readers of the future.

We'd love you to think of sharing, borrowing, reading, buying
or talking about a book with a child in your life and spreading
the love of reading. We want to make sure the next generation
continue to have access to books, wherever they come from.

And if you would like to consider donating to charities
that help fund literacy projects, find out more at
www.literacytrust.org.uk and **www.booktrust.org.uk**.

THANK YOU

*As reported by the National Literacy Trust

Permissions